D1397504

Teardrop Headlights

Benjamin Moore

Divine Impressions

Austin, Texas

Published by Divine Impressions.
Address inquiries to the publisher or author at
PO Box 52
Plum, Texas 78952
Email: publisher@teardropheadlights.com
www. teardropheadlights.com

Cover images:

Benjamin Moore, age 3, and his dog Blaze from the author's collection.

International Harvester Metro photograph by Cheri Lomonte.

Benjamin Moore photo by Tom Etter, Etter Photography.

Book cover and design by Sheila Setter.

Scripture texts in this work are taken from the Holy Bible, King James Version (KJV) and New King James Version (NKJV) and verified at Bible Gateway (https://www.biblegateway.com).

Printed in the United States of America.

ISBN-13: 978-1545443491
ISBN-10: 1545443491

Teardrop Headlights

DEDICATION

For all those children who had no voice.

Contents

Contents

TEARDROP
HEADLIGHTS

1

The Calling

Tioga County, New York, is in one of the most picturesque areas of the United States. The Susquehanna River lazily splits rolling hills as it works its way south from the Finger Lakes region down through New York State and Pennsylvania to the Chesapeake Bay. The hills are covered with hardwood forests of sugar maple, oak, ash, and ironwood along with spruce, pine, and other evergreens that create a spectacular palette of color in the fall. In the spring, splashes of dogwood blossoms complement the view. There are fields on many hillsides dotted with feeding cattle and horses and the occasional John Deere tractor, and it seems every valley has a barn with a matching silo and farmhouse nearby.

Guy D. Moore and his wife Georgia Pearl worked this land. It had been passed down through my family all the way back to the Revolutionary War when it was awarded to my direct ancestor, Nathaniel Moore, for his service to our new nation.

Grandpa was a small man, but tough. In his younger years, he had been a boxer who built a reputation after knocking an opponent through the second-story window of the establishment where bouts were held. He was also a plumber, a small town politician, and a dairy farmer. Grandma was a school teacher, a wife, and a mother.

Grandma and Grandpa had ten children. Dad was the second oldest and the oldest boy. He talked about being able to "work like a man" by the time he was fourteen. Early on in Dad's youth, Grandpa made a deal with him: if he worked the farm and helped put his younger brothers and sisters through college, he and my uncles, Paul and Bob, would inherit the farm. It was very successful—at any given time milking approximately seventy registered Holsteins.

Dad kept his word and so did Grandpa. After serving his time in WWII, Dad came home, met and married

Patricia Ann Bradley, took a hundred-acre chunk of fertile family farmland overlooking the Susquehanna, and settled down. If you stand in one spot in a back field, you can see fifteen miles downriver towards Waverly, New York. This is where the first five of his children, including me, were born. It was on this land and during this time that Dad received "The Calling."

As Dad told the story, in the evening after the cows were milked and supper was over, he would get his beer and some popcorn and stretch out on the floor to read his Bible. One night, he had a dream; and in this dream, he was in heaven. Everything was bright; the temperature perfect; the angels sang songs of praise. There was no sadness or sorrow or tears. Dad was at peace with himself and everyone. He was home.

The next night, he had the same dream. And the night after. He dreamed a similar dream five nights in a row. In each dream, he saw new wonders. During his dream on the fifth night, he said to God, "This is really beautiful, but what does it have to do with *me?*" At that moment, his dream abruptly ended; he never had it again.

He told this story many times. Each time, he would cry, tears dripping down his nose. He regretted for the rest of his life having asked that question.

Shortly thereafter, he decided to go to seminary school. I think he realized he would have to earn that dream the hard way.

Dad sold the farm for about a third of its value. He got an old 1939 International Harvester Metro panel truck, complete with "teardrop headlights," and built out the insides with a bottom and top bunk. He added a little partition where he installed "The Pot," an old five-gallon grease can we could use as a bathroom. Then to complete the project, he mounted a giant loudspeaker on the back and hand-painted signs on the sides and back that read, "Repent, for the Kingdom of heaven is at hand!" and "If you are not willing to leave your father and mother for me, you are not worthy of me!"

When the Old Truck was ready, Dad loaded us up. Dan was eight, Althea five, I was three, Ruth was two, and Martha was less than a year old. Mom and our old farm dog Pepper completed the ensemble.

The Old Truck had a top speed of 45 mph; and in 1959, the freeway system was yet to be built.

It took us ten days to get to Texas.

2

The Texas Soul Clinic

The Texas Soul Clinic was located outside of Thurber, a dusty ghost town surrounded by mesquite and scrub brush about seventy-five miles west of Fort Worth. It was dry and hot—a natural home for armadillos, scorpions, and rattlesnakes. The Soul Clinic had been founded in the early 1950s by Fred Jordan, an evangelist who had inherited the four-hundred-acre ranch from his mother.

TSC was basically a circular drive with cabins on each side and a mess hall at the end. According to Linda Davis, author of *The Children of God—The Inside Story*, "Fred had designed the ranch to serve as a boot camp training center for prospective missionaries enrolled in his Soul Clinic program. He determined that if potential missionaries could make it at the Texas Soul Clinic, they could no doubt survive quite well on a foreign field." Later on, it would become the headquarters for the Children of God, a cult built by David Berg, an associate of Fred Jordan's. It was a place where men learned to witness, preach, and raise money, and women took care of the cooking and cleaning.

Dad would get all riled up when he talked about our time there. Apparently, he was not well received. Although he claimed he had a 108 grade-point average, he was kicked out of the school and asked to leave the premises. He said Fred Jordan, who also taught Bible classes, told him he guessed even the devil could get good grades. Mom once said of those times, "Your father was a true Protestant—he protested everything!"

What I remember of our time there are little glimpses: playing baseball and getting hit on the head with a bat; standing on a Texas red ant hill and not realizing it until it was too late; getting spanked for throwing my green beans under my chair; walking along the road with Althea early on a Saturday morning; singing "Sweeter as the Years Go By" on the loudspeaker for someone's birthday; Dick Whittington's plane flying steeply into the sky; counting to seven hundred before

I could fall sleep; Dan and I being told to go get some pears, then knocking them all off the tree and getting in trouble for doing it; adults standing around during a tornado watch while I wondered why they weren't terrified like I was; falling off the top bunk and hitting my head on the concrete floor; a bunch of us kids going into an empty cabin, taking our clothes off, and jumping naked on the bed...and spankings—always the spankings. Apparently, I was an unruly child.

Dad sometimes said to Mom, "Patty, we're gonna have to break these kids."

I also recall bits and pieces of a trip out to Fred Jordan's Skid Row Mission in Los Angeles, California, and standing out on the street corners while the men went and ministered to the drunks, hippies, and bums. At one point, I heard a bottle break; and when I asked what that was, an adult answered, "That was a drunk accepting Jesus."

We finally left TSC with Dad fuming. It became a familiar scene to be somewhere where there was food and fellowship, only to be suddenly on the road with Dad ranting and Mom saying, "Yes, Dear....No, Dear....I understand...."

3

Peanut Butter Sandwiches

We were on the road again, this time, headed for Mexico. The trip from Thurber to the Rio Grande Valley was hot and lonely. Toward evening, we stopped at a roadside park outside of Weslaco, Texas. It had been a long day. Everyone was hungry, cranky, and tired. We sat in a circle while Dad put a dollop of peanut butter on a slice of bread for each of us kids.

This was our supper.

When I got my piece, I whined, "Mine doesn't have enough peanut butter!"

Dad took it back, cupped it in his hand, and slammed it into my face. I soon had blood pouring out of my nose, which mixed nicely with the peanut butter and bread. I was now squalling.

Dad turned to Mom and said, "Clean him up."

I made many decisions in that instant: *I am bad. Don't ever complain to Dad again. I don't matter.* Up to that point, everything had been pretty OK. That moment, however, was a turning point. It was my fall from grace. From then on, my life took on a much darker cast.

After awhile, Dad said to Mom, "Love him a little."

⌁⌁⌁

That night, we slept in the Old Truck—all seven of us and Pepper our dog. Not a breeze was stirring, and it was very hot. I laid there between Dan and Dad; and I was so miserable, I could barely stand it. I longed for a way to cool off. I was supposed to be still, but I couldn't stop fidgeting. I was frightened by the strange sounds coming from the outside, and Dad felt like a furnace next to me. He was so big that he blocked any breeze that might come my way.

I put my bare feet against the inside of the truck to feel the coolness, but it only made me feel hotter. I imagined a little battery-powered fan that I could put on my chest so it would blow just a little air on my face; but of course, there was no fan.

It was just hot.

Presently, some teenagers pulled into the park. I suppose they were drinking. They were very loud in the stillness of the night; we could hear them clearly, every word they said, as they laughed and boasted. Soon they took notice of the Old Truck with the loudspeaker on top and the Jesus signs carefully hand painted on the sides, and they began calling out and making fun of us. They got closer and closer until they were right outside our truck, shaking the bicycle we had strapped to the back and yelling.

I was afraid.

After about ten minutes of this, Dad had enough. He got up, put his pants on, and slowly began to open the sliding door.

The hoodlums immediately ran off. Dad yelled after them, "Come on back! You forgot your guts!"

He was very upset with himself after that. He explained that he shouldn't have lost his temper, and we should be tolerant of others—even when they clearly harassed us and were in the wrong.

After that, we were pretty wound up; but eventually, we went to sleep.

4

Mexico

Due to my young age, our first trip into Mexico is still pretty vague. I was somewhere between four and five years old.

We had never been to Mexico, and Dad didn't yet know about *la mordida*—"the bite"—but by golly, after the first trip, every time we crossed the border, Dad would stop somewhere before getting to the international bridge to change a twenty into one dollar bills. Then we would cross into Mexico and pull up to the *Oficina de Aduanales* (customs office) to apply for a six-month visa.

All the *aduanal* officials wore chocolate-brown uniforms. They would get up from where they were sitting, their sweat-stained uniforms looking like salty road maps, and amble over to check out the contents of the Old Truck. Then they would hem and haw and poke and prod until Dad handed them each a dollar bill.

You didn't really want to hand over the cash too soon or appear too eager because then it was obviously a bribe, and they'd wonder what you were hiding. But once they looked through your stuff the appropriate amount of time, a dollar became a tip or *propina*. If you waited too long to give them la mordida, they would get irritated and search your stuff just to annoy you. However, if you did it just right and they figured they had gotten as much as they were gonna get, they would nod their heads and amble off again.

Occasionally, some guy in a cowboy hat and huaraches would drift over and start poking through our stuff. If the guys in the brown uniforms shooed him away, we'd ignore him. If they didn't, we'd give him a dollar, too. Once everyone had their "bite" and that shiny decal was attached to our windshield, we were free to go.

On each Mexican highway, twenty kilometers in, was another aduanal stop. There, we would point to our sticker, show our visa papers to the *agentes*, and go through the same routine. As long as we had enough dollar bills, we were good.

On this trip, we ended up in Ciudad Mante, a fairly large town in the state of Tamaulipas. What I remember most about this place is the sugar cane trucks—old, rickety, smoking jalopies loaded with green, red, yellow, and purple sugar cane laboring down the unpaved streets toward the sugar factory.

When we arrived, the first thing we did was find the central plaza and park. A small crowd was hanging around; and when someone got the urge, he would jump up, run after a passing truck, grab hold of a cane, and pull. Sugar cane must have been the original candy cane because after the cane came free, he would carry his prize back to his buddies; and they would pull out their pocketknives and machetes and peel and chew on the cane, spitting pulp as they chewed until all the sweetness was gone.

Mexico is predominately Catholic, and Mexican Catholics disdained anyone who wasn't one of them, so we inquired around until we found a member of *los aleluyas* (the Hallelujahs). Anyone who wasn't Catholic was considered an aleluya, whether they were Baptist, Lutheran, or Pentecostal; and since we weren't Catholic, we fell in the aleluya category.

We landed at a family's house, which was nothing more than a shack, and parked the Old Truck in their yard for a few days. We were treated like visiting dignitaries.

Mexican people are very generous, and this family felt obliged to feed us, so they decided to go deer hunting. Deer hunting among the poor people in Mexico is done in the dark with a good, strong flashlight and a .22 long rifle. That night, we went to bed in the Old Truck; and the next morning, the hunters came home with a small, dressed deer. They gave us some of the meat; and although Dad grumbled to us that they hadn't dressed it properly, we fried it up and ate it. Fresh meat was a treat for us, and it was delicious.

Later that day, I had my first burro ride. It was clear this little gray burro wanted nothing to do with me because as soon as I was mounted, she headed for the nearest low-hanging tree branch and did her best to scrape me off. Eventually, she scrubbed me up against the stick fence until I fell off and she was free.

I guess we ended up renting a little place for a few days because I remember a house with several rooms, each one painted a different pastel color. Mom got out the old camp stove and cooked tortillas and French fries. Dad had bought a tortilla press, which consisted of two flat, cast-iron disks about eight inches in diameter held together with a hinge. The contraption was complete with a lever, which also had a hinge. The idea was to roll a ball of *masa* (corn meal dough) about the size of a golf ball and place it on the bottom disk, fold the upper disk over the top, and then push down the lever to flatten the masa ball into a tortilla.

We didn't know you were supposed to use plastic wrap or wax paper on the two disks so the masa wouldn't stick to the press, and neither did we understand that we were supposed to put the raw tortillas on a hot griddle to cook them. We just cooked them in the press, which was very slow going. The tortillas ended up burned more often than not, and they came off the press in chunks. We didn't much like them, but of course we had to eat them anyway. Eventually, Dad struck a deal with us: for every tortilla we ate, we got a handful of fries. After that, everyone was happy.

I guess this was a fact-finding mission because after a few weeks, we headed back to the United States. I'll never forget the tension rising the closer we got to the border—Mom was a worrier, and she wrung her hands a lot. The Mexican side waved us through, of course, since we were leaving the country. We were then searched on the US side and asked questions about whether or not we had brought in any fruit or plants. Mom answered the best she could with a terrified look on her face. Meanwhile, I felt guilty because I was used to being a bad kid, and no telling what I had done. *Did I, by chance, put a plant somewhere in the truck? Or fruit?*

Of course, we didn't attempt to bribe the American customs officials; and eventually, we were on our way.

I'll never forget how glad I was to be back on US soil. Everything looked green, the lawns were trimmed and tended, the highways were smooth and wide, people spoke English, and we didn't have to fear the police.

I wanted to kiss the ground.

5

Lake Leon

After our first trip to Mexico, Dad decided we should go back to the Texas Soul Clinic for a visit.

Along the way, one of our stops was near a lake in a desolate area of West Texas. Lake Leon.

I enjoyed going to lakes. For one thing, there was the possibility of fishing, which I loved to do. Fried fish provided a break from the bashed canned goods we mostly lived on when we were on the road. There was also the possibility of swimming, giving us a break from the heat. I had learned to swim in a creek in Del Rio a few months before, and it was new and exciting fun.

We arrived at Lake Leon and unloaded the camp stove, ice chest, and fishing gear. While Mom set up the stove on a cement picnic table, we explored the boat ramp, which was nothing more than a shallow cove with a sandy bottom.

We asked Dad if we could swim, and he said no. He told us we could pull up our pant legs and wade, but no swimming. The water felt cool as we waded around, and soon our pants were wet all the way up to our waists.

Why not swim?

Soon we were frolicking around splashing each other and having a great time—and swimming.

Mom took notice first and let out a shriek. Then Dad yelled as he came out of the truck. Soon he was ordering us out of the water. We were in deep trouble, and we knew it. He was so angry that he promised each of us a spanking. He said he was going to spank Mom, too, because she had allowed us to swim in the first place.

Now I *knew* I was a bad boy. I clearly heard him say we were not to swim; yet somehow, I had ended up swimming anyway. But it wasn't Mom's fault, and I felt ashamed for her. And I hated Dad for including her with us disobedient children.

We waited all day for a spanking. I kept wishing he would go ahead and punish us and get it over with so we could go have some fun.

He never did.

It was the longest day of my life.

6

Cool, Clear Water

I was about six when we moved to Los Herreras, a little village in northern Mexico, about fifty miles from Monterrey. Mexico in the late 1950s was pretty primitive. Most little villages, even county seats like this one, had only one or two TVs, which were owned by the "rich" people in town. And while many had electricity, no one had running water. Anything new coming into a little village was cause for unabashed gawking and hooting.

As we pulled into town, a crowd began to gather. Children ran excitedly beside the Old Truck, which in addition to the large loudspeaker mounted on the top was adorned on the back and both sides with Christian messages.

We slowly worked our way down the unpaved streets to the far end of the village, turned on a side street across from the cemetery, and parked at the curb.

It was very hot. The Old Truck didn't have windows so we opened the side and back doors to let in some air. It was still unbearable.

By now, a crowd had assembled around us, and everyone was jabbering and pointing and jostling for position. We didn't understand a thing they were saying, and we didn't get out. We just sat in the truck in the hot sun for a very long time. With nothing new to see, the crowd began slowly moving away. A few of the kids retired to a safe distance to resume their card game, but they kept an eye on the truck in case something exciting happened.

Eventually, a grimy little girl holding an earthen jar of ice water timidly approached the Old Truck. As she fearfully came toward us, she held up her offering—a typical welcome gesture in rural Mexico. Dad turned her down, sending her back with the cold water still in her little hands. My mouth watered with thirst, but my face burned with shame. I couldn't understand how he could be so rude.

Years later, I mentioned the incident to Mom. She remembered it and exclaimed, "Your father was just trying to keep us from getting diarrhea!"

7

Escuela

Shortly after we arrived in Los Herreras, we rented a two-room house, complete with a well, cistern, and back porch. The walls around the backyard were made of cinder blocks and in typical Mexican fashion, topped with jagged shards of broken glass set in concrete. This discouraged dogs and people from scaling the wall. The walls were flanked by castor bean bushes, and we had great fun using the dried stalks for drinking straws until we all got sick.

To furnish our living quarters, Dad went to the local store and bought cinder blocks and boards. With these supplies, he made raised beds, a kitchen table, and a platform for Mom's camp stove. We had no refrigerator, no air conditioning, and like the rest of the village, no running water. These were considered luxuries in poor Mexican villages, and very few people had them. There were no locks on the doors and no screens on the windows. Instead, there were steel bars. But after months of living in the truck, we finally had a home.

After we were settled, Dad enrolled us in school. I was put in the second grade because that was the last grade I had attended in Nichols, New York. It was then that my hell began.

No one at the school spoke English, and I didn't know a word of Spanish, so I had no idea what was happening at any given time. I understood nothing that was being spoken, either inside the classroom or out. But I was good at math because 32 − 12 = 20 in any language. And since I excelled in the subject, the teachers took a liking to me and would take the time to pick up a pencil, point to it, and say, "La-*peece*. La-*peece*."

I stuck close to those teachers as much as I could. They taught me Spanish and provided a bit of safety. They also decided I was very cute and would pinch me on the cheeks with their eagle-like claws saying, "*Ay, que chulo!* (Oh, how cute!)" I wore marks on my cheeks daily.

But the teachers weren't the *real* problem.

My classmates were.

Recess was particularly frightening. The kids would surround me in a circle in the back of the schoolyard, prod me with sticks, and shout, *"Gringo Palote, te sumo el garrote!"* which roughly means, "Skinny gringo, I'm gonna shove this stick up your ass!" I had no idea at the time what they were saying. I was simply terrified. I could not run, and I could not fight, so I just took it.

On my second day in school, I stooped down to get a drink from the water fountain, which happened to be running at the moment. When I straightened up, I caught a boy's fist square in the mouth. I bled all over, but I didn't fight back. I had already been warned about fighting by my father. "Turn the other cheek!" he would say.

I don't know if I didn't fight back because of that or because I was a coward, but I soon got used to backing down from most fights. Fifty years later, I still have the lump from that fight inside my bottom lip. I can feel it with my tongue. *Funny how some scars never heal.*

When I came home with scratches or bruises from fighting, Dad's first question was always, "Did you turn the other cheek?"

If I hadn't, I was whipped right there on the spot.

If I had, I was praised.

If I had fought but lied about it, I would get undeserved praise. This was worse than being punished. I was damned for lying, and I knew it.

I learned to pick my fights. I never started them; but when provoked, if I thought I could take the other kid without a scratch, I would. Mostly, though, I just got beat up. I was ashamed.

In my neighborhood, we had gangs. *Gangs*—at the age of *six*! I still don't know how some of us came to be in one gang and others in another. It wasn't divided geographically or racially. It was more like we chose which team we were on; and if accepted, we did violence on the other. We would stalk and attack each other with our fists, slingshots, and BB guns. I didn't have a BB gun, but I was getting good at using my fists. I would hide in an abandoned building and wait for someone from the enemy gang to walk by. Once I ambushed a kid by jumping out in front of him and hitting him right in the mouth. The punch was perfectly executed with a long follow through. He went down like a sack of grain. I'll never forget that feeling of power. I suppose most wars start that way—for no good reason.

Sometimes Dad and I would stand on the street corner and proclaim the Word in Spanish. I didn't know

Spanish, of course, but Dad would make me read La Biblia anyway. "Just read it," he'd say. So I'd read and read, not understanding a word I was saying; and there would be circles of kids around me, jeering and laughing and making fun of me.

At some point in the fourth grade, I began understanding a little Spanish. Dad always said, "If you ever dream in Spanish, you will have learned Spanish," and one night, sure enough, I did.

I had always been good in school, usually second or third in my class—but that was in English-speaking schools. After that dream, I started getting pretty good grades in Los Herreras.

One day, I came home from school with my report card and proudly showed off my straight As to Dad.

He thought very little of schoolwork and told me, "Education is of the devil; you should put your eyes on Jesus."

Looking back, I suspect one of the reasons I got good grades was to spite him.

8

Sacred Pursuits

In 1962, the Houston Colt .45s became an expansion team for Major League Baseball's National League. Several years later, after NASA's moon launches, the team changed their name to the Houston Astros.

Dan had a small transistor radio; and at night, we could listen to KTRH, their blowtorch flag station, clear down into the northern part of Mexico. It is impossible to exaggerate how important the Colt .45s were to Dan and me. Here we were immersed in a culture we were unfamiliar with, eating food we didn't like, listening to a language we were still learning to understand. We were homesick and lonely. But every night, the Colt .45s' broadcast came on with the sonorous tones of their announcer Gene Elston.

Baseball was my home away from home, and Mexico was big on baseball. The nearest city with a professional team was Monterrey. The team was called *Los Sultanes*; and their big star was Hector Espino, who was known to have crushed a home run 520 feet from home plate. He played in the Major Leagues for a short time but reportedly got homesick and went back home.

On a local level, we played baseball all the time. No one in those small towns could afford real baseballs or bats, so we had to make the equipment ourselves. The bats were usually made of mesquite, and we made baseballs by wrapping rubber balls with electrical tape until they were big enough. If you had a glove or a real bat or ball, you could always get in a game even if you weren't any good because the kids, well, they needed your equipment.

I finally got a glove one year. It was a Rawlings fielder's glove. I put saddle soap on that thing every week. I would put the glove over my face and smell the leather and slap a baseball over and over into it to form the pocket. I bent it and worked it until I got it just right. I loved that glove more than anything I had ever owned.

And that glove got me playing time because when my team was batting, the other team had my glove.

⁓❦⁓

I learned to play soccer and other games like tops and marbles and cards with the kids in my village, but it was my dad who taught me a lesson about playing that has lasted my lifetime.

We were still living in that little house in Los Herreras when Dad taught me how to play checkers. At first, of course, he beat me every time. He was very generous with his play and showed me when I made errors and taught me how to trap my opponent and plan three or four moves ahead.

I enjoyed these games with Dad—they were rare times when every conversation didn't turn into a talk about God, something I had a constant complaint about.

One day, I beat him. I was so proud of myself; and he was proud of me, too. We played many times after that, and I got better and better until I was winning a fair number of games.

By the time I was eight, he rarely won a game.

I became arrogant, quietly gloating when I would set my trap. When he would fall for it, I would snap it shut, and being one up, trade checker for checker until he conceded.

One day, I asked him to play, and he said no.

I was disappointed and a little mystified and asked him why he didn't want to play.

He said, in fact, he didn't want to play me at all anymore—he didn't like the way he felt toward me when I won.

We never played checkers again.

9

More School

We went back to New York that summer. In the fall, I enrolled in Nichols Elementary School.

I should have gone to the third grade; however, the principal, Mr. Novak, decided to hold me back a year.

I watched all my classmates go to the third grade classroom while I stayed in second grade. I was embarrassed and ashamed. I knew, given half a chance, I could do the third grade schoolwork, and I had passed from second to third in Mexico.

But I was flunked.

I wanted to shout to my classmates that I was at least as smart if not smarter than they were, and I wanted to explain to Mr. Novak that I *could* do the work. But I wasn't given the opportunity. And I was very shy. The decision was made, and I had nothing to say about it.

That ate at me for years. The irony of the story is I suppose I got the last laugh. Nine years later, I enrolled in the twelfth grade and graduated with my original classmates. By then, however, no one remembered I had flunked second grade, and I no longer cared.

⚜

Every day during the week before Christmas break, they announced over the intercom that the school was planning a turkey dinner with mashed potatoes and gravy. We were told to bring money for it. We would be celebrating before going on vacation.

I wanted so badly to have that Christmas lunch, but I knew Dad would never spring for it. We never had money for school lunches. We had peanut butter and jelly sandwiches in brown paper bags.

Since we were the only kids who hadn't brought any money for the Christmas lunch, Mr. Novak let us eat for free.

That same year, my second grade class had a Secret Santa activity. We each put our name on a little piece of paper, folded it up, and put it in a hat. Then we drew names. Whichever name we drew was the classmate we had to bring a present for. I don't remember whose name I drew; and of course, I didn't know who had drawn my name.

On the day of the party, I sat next to Chucky Wiswold on the school bus. He was carrying his wrapped present, and I was curious about what it was. I guess I was kind of bossy because even though he wouldn't say who the present was for, I did talk him into unwrapping it so I could see it. It was a set of Lincoln Logs, which I thought was a pretty dumb present, and I told him so.

A few hours later, we exchanged gifts. I got an unwrapped set of Lincoln Logs.

I loved being in school in Nichols. Although we were poor and wore hand-me-downs while other kids wore nice school clothes, I felt normal. I always got straight As there…and it was one place where I got positive re-enforcement from adults.

One day for some reason, Mr. Novak was teaching our second grade class. He asked who could spell "lion."

I raised my hand and shouted, "L-O-I-N!"

All the kids laughed, and I was embarrassed. However, Mr. Novak shushed them saying, "No, no, no, children! *Loin* is a real word! It's a cut of meat!"

I knew I had spelled it wrong, but I was grateful he had allowed me to save face.

I guess Mr. Novak wasn't so bad after all.

10

Learning to Beg

We lived in Los Herreras on and off for several years. I say on and off because we would often pack up and head to the States or even to Grandma's house in New York. Sometimes we would just drive somewhere and stop for a few weeks or months for no apparent reason. None of us kids dared to ask Dad where we were going, what we were doing, or how long we would be there. We were just *there*. If it was in the States and we were somewhere long enough, we would enroll in the nearest school for a couple of weeks. Then we'd be on the road again.

When we weren't in Mexico, we spent a lot of time sitting in roadside parks...waiting. Staying in touch with

Grandma in those days was almost impossible, but we communicated via the US mail. When we were traveling, Grandma didn't know where to send our checks; so we would call collect, have her mail a check to General Delivery in whatever small town we were near, and then wait for it to arrive.

We would sit in roadside parks and watch people come and eat; and as soon as their car was out of sight, we'd run to the garbage cans to see what they'd left. It always amazed me how much food people wasted.

Sometimes they would leave a watermelon with only the middle gone. We would eat the rest. At times, whole sandwiches with exotic meats like bologna and salami were left behind. Or maybe some pie. Whatever it was, it would all be included in our supper.

Occasionally, someone would have a barbecue at one of these parks. I could smell the meat roasting, and it would make my stomach growl. If they had kids, it was easy for us to work ourselves in. We would just start playing with the kids. Next thing you know, when the food was ready, we'd be handed a plate!

It was a little more difficult when there were no kids. I got really good at hanging around close and "looking hungry." It wasn't hard to do. We *were* hungry.

If we didn't get invited, then they always left something behind that we could eat.

When we weren't begging or "looking hungry" at roadside parks, if there was a creek nearby, we would try to catch fish or hunt for soda bottles in the ditches. Back then, you could get a nickel apiece for soda bottles—enough for a candy bar or a bag of peanuts and a Dr. Pepper at the gas station.

Once, we found three unopened beer cans. We took them to Dad, who promptly ordered us to destroy them. We shook them up and punctured them on a barbed wire fence. We had great fun spraying warm beer all over the place. Mom's only comment was, "What a waste."

When we went to a grocery store, the first thing we would do is go to the back and find all the damaged canned goods. Often they were unidentifiable because the labels had fallen off, but these constituted a major source of our meals. Many a time after a long day of travel, we circled around the trunk of the car watching Mom open bashed-in cans to see what we were having for supper. Sometimes it would be dog food, in which case Pepper was happy. In most cases, it was people food, and that was our meal. Occasionally, we would catch a grocery store special like Mellorine, three half gallons for a dollar. Then we would eat imitation ice cream till our foreheads ached. During one of our forays into a grocery store, Dad found two cases of creamed carrots in the damaged food cart. To this day, I can't eat a cooked carrot.

⸺❦⸺

The practice of enrolling in and out of schools was standard fare for us growing up. It was not unusual for us to attend three or four schools—some in Mexico and some in the United States—during the course of a school year. By now, I could switch from English to a Spanish-speaking curriculum on a dime.

I was an avid reader. Mom boasted that she taught me to read at the age of four, and reading became one of my escapes from the difficult circumstances in which we lived our lives. Dad permitted us to read only certain things: the Bible, *Reader's Digest*, The Reader's Digest Condensed Books, and our textbooks.

When we left a school, we always kept our textbooks, and I would read them over and over. It wasn't that I was trying to stay ahead in school—I was simply bored. Often we would be out of school for two months, land somewhere, enroll in school, and I could be caught up with my classmates within two or three weeks.

When we camped at Bentsen-Rio Grande Valley State Park, we attended school in La Joya, Texas. Every morning, the school bus picked us up right in the park. I was enrolled there in fourth grade, and a lot of my classmates were immigrant kids who spoke only Spanish. By now, my Spanish was pretty good; so occasionally, I would converse with them in their native language. The teachers were attempting to force all the students to speak English, and immigrant kids were expected to learn quickly. As an incentive, they got spanked if they were caught speaking Spanish. I got paddled right along with them.

That school year, I made a new friend. His name was Timmy, and he was great fun. It felt very strange to be in the relative opulence of the Rio Grande Valley after spending most of my time in Mexico, and one thing I noticed was that Timmy and a lot of the other kids had toys. *Real* toys—not the kind we made in Mexico or the cheap kind made out of wood. No, these were shiny, colorful toys made out of real plastic and metal.

Timmy had a rocket with fins and a nose made of metal. If you loaded it with caps, like a cap gun, and hurled it to the ground, it would sound off with a loud crack.

I loved it, and Timmy gave it to me.

After awhile, he wanted it back.

I'd never had anything like it, and I refused to give it back to him. We argued until he offered to give me a quarter for it. That was a lot of money in the early 1960s, so I took it.

A short time later, the teacher came by and took the money away from me and gave it back to Timmy. It seemed to me that I had once again been cheated out of the material side of life; and if ever I got anything of value, it would soon be taken away.

11

Wild Locusts & Honey, Manna & Money

M ost of the time, we were living on the road. I will always be grateful to Grandma, Uncle Paul, and Uncle Dick for sending us money. Between the three, we received up to $175 a month. This is what we lived on; although, Althea says it was usually much less than that.

Dad would not work regular jobs. He said, "A workman is worthy of his meat," and Dad's work was the ministry, so when we ran out of money, we just made do. He used to brag that "we never missed a meal." Perhaps some of our meals *should* have been missed.

Once we were totally out of food and money. We were sitting at a roadside park as we often did when we didn't have any particular place to go. On this day, there were grasshoppers everywhere. Large, fat ones. Dad reasoned that John the Baptist ate locusts and wild honey; so we could, too. We had great fun catching them, pulling their heads off, and putting them into a big frying pan. After we had filled up the pan, Dad ordered Mom to cook them up, and she did.

When we sat down to eat, Dad told me to ask the blessing. I did. I thanked God for the food. When I said "Amen," Dad said, "Eat!"

I refused.

"Ask the blessing again," he ordered.

I did, once more thanking God for our food. When I said, "Amen," he said, "Eat!"

I refused again.

"Ask the blessing again!"

I could see where this was going, so I ate a few of the grasshoppers. It was not our best meal.

Years later when I would tell this story, occasionally someone would ask, "Well, how were they?"

I would say, "Not bad. Kinda crunchy."

Then one day, my friend Tom said, "Oh, really? Have you eaten any since?"

To which I could only reply, "No."

"Well, they couldn't have been *that* good," he said.

I have since learned from reading the Essene New Testament (one of the old manuscripts unearthed with the Dead Sea Scrolls) that John the Baptist was a vegetarian and ate "the *fruit* of the *honey locust tree.*"

Big difference.

⁓⁂⁓

Once when we were getting very low on cash, I overheard Dad and Mom discussing our situation. Dad said we had only $1.61 left. We were somewhere in Texas waiting for Grandma's check, and we were afraid and desperate.

Dad said, "God will provide."

Later that day, we stopped at a roadside park. All of a sudden, Dan started finding money! A quarter here, a dime there, and each time, Dad would exclaim loudly, "Praise the Lord!"

We were all pretty excited, and now we were all looking for money. Somehow, though, Dan was the only one who was finding any. When Dad counted out the amount Dan had found, it amounted to exactly $1.61.

And the original $1.61 was nowhere to be found.

We fell deeper into despair.

12

Fish Tales

When we crossed into the States to renew our visas, we often stayed at the Bentsen-Rio Grande Valley State Park. On this particular visit, the lake was up, and it had flooded the trees up past the brush line so there was no way to get out very far except by boat. We, of course, didn't have one.

I was fishing from the boat ramp using a rod and reel, hoping to get my bait out to the deeper water. I was accustomed to fishing for bluegill, perch, crappie, and catfish in Mexico using cane poles or fishing line rolled up on tin cans, but I hadn't yet fished much with this kind of tackle.

Two largemouth bass were lazily patrolling the area right off the ramp; but they weren't interested in anything I threw out there with a hook, bobber, and sinker. In fact, when I tried getting their attention, the splash of the rigging startled them. I didn't have any bass lures, so it looked like we were going without fish that night.

Then I had an idea. I took the bobber and sinker off the line, leaving only the hook. Looking around for something to use as bait, I spotted a cricket and put it on the hook. I pulled some line off the spool like a fly fisherman, waded out as far as I dared without spooking the fish, and sort of tossed the hooked cricket out toward the fish.

It landed lightly right above the two bass and BAM! They EXPLODED under that cricket. One of them was hooked on my line, and I was hooked on bass fishing.

It wasn't a huge fish—maybe two pounds—but it was much bigger than the pan fish we were used to catching. It actually needed to be filleted to be cooked. This was a breakthrough in my ability to catch fish for dinner.

For the next two weeks, Dan and I fished that lake every chance we got. Since there was no access to the water from the shoreline, we started wading out beyond the brush into the open water. At some points, it would get too deep, and we'd swim with one arm while holding our rods and reels over our heads with the other so they wouldn't get wet. Once we arrived at a new spot, we could stand and cast at submerged brush or logs; dangle crickets, worms, or grasshoppers down into little openings in the brush; and often haul out a nice fish.

Until then, Dad had never been much interested in fishing in earnest as a source of food, but even he started getting into it. He reasoned that several of Jesus's disciples were fishermen, so it was an honorable profession. Sitting around the campfire after dinner, he would contentedly say, "Kings don't eat any better than this!"

Another lake we frequented was Lake Sam Rayburn in East Texas. I loved that lake. It is set in the piney woods; and for some reason, the trees reminded me of home. We spent a fair amount of time there because lakes where the Army Corps of Engineers had built dams always had free camping areas. The only stipulation for staying was that you had to move every two weeks. If we were going to be in the States for awhile, we'd move from one campsite to the next. We could go indefinitely in this manner and never pay a dime in camping fees; and since we used a

Coleman stove and lanterns, we didn't need electricity so we were able to make our money stretch.

I fished barefoot, wading out waist-deep, casting my lures next to logs and branches. While the "real" fishermen went roaring across the lake in their fancy bass boats to catch the big ones, I'd stay close by, catching nice bass—sometimes even in the coves they had just left.

One day, I found a silver and white redfin, a top-water lure, washed up on the shore. I put it on, and it quickly became my favorite. I could expertly cast it to just the right spot, let it rest for a minute, and give it a little twitch. *Bam! Fish on!* The water would boil while I brought in my catch, and on my stringer it went!

I loved fishing like this. It allowed me to get away from the campsite and Dad and explore the lakes on my own. And sometimes, I'd come across soda bottles, which I could get a nickel apiece for, so it afforded me my share of Pay Days and Dr. Peppers.

Occasionally, I'd come across a cottonmouth, but they usually kept their distance, and I stayed away from them, too. One day, however, I was fishing about a half mile from camp, walking along the shoreline, looking for a good place to wade in. Just as I stepped into the water, I noticed a huge, writhing ball underwater.

It was about a foot in diameter. At first, I couldn't tell what it was; but as it slowly came into focus, I realized it was a ball of water moccasins engaged in some kind of slow, hypnotic dance. The hair stood up on the back of my neck, and I slowly backed out of there before they noticed me.

Another time I was fishing in water a little above my waist. It had rained recently, which usually meant good fishing because there was a lot of food—worms and bugs—washing into the lake. Out of the corner of my eye, I kept noticing these leaves floating, and they had a reddish hue. I didn't pay much attention until I brushed up against one. It turned out to be a floating leaf covered with fire ants. And they were swarming *everywhere*. The next thing I knew, they were in my pants and under my shirt, biting the fire out of me!

But a bad day of fishing is still better than a good day anywhere else, and these were minor complications. I loved fishing, and I fished every chance I got.

13

Becoming a Man

Toward the end of my fifth year in school, Dad moved our family from Los Herreras to Los Ramones, the next town upriver. Althea, Ruth, and I enrolled in the Escuela Primaria Don Miguel Hidalgo—Althea moved into sixth grade, I went into fifth, and Ruth into fourth. Dan enrolled in the first-ever seventh grade in that small town's Escuela Secundaria Don Benito Juarez. Up until that year, sixth grade was the highest grade taught in that town. Prior to that, no one had ever considered an education beyond the sixth grade to be important. Dan was one of twenty-nine students.

As we progressed through the school system, Dan eventually graduated from ninth grade with a high school diploma. Althea graduated the next year, and I graduated the third year. Eventually, I transferred my grades from ninth grade in Mexico to twelfth grade in Tioga County, New York, and graduated there.

My Spanish was now passable, and I was making straight As in my coursework. I wasn't getting bullied quite as much, and I began developing friendships—the most important one being with Carlos Navarro. Carlos was one of thirteen kids. He and his family lived in the house directly across the back wall from the three-room house we rented. His dad, Don Julio, was the *Secretario del Alcalde* (secretary to the mayor) of Los Ramones. This meant he was the acting mayor under the elected mayor, who was a figurehead with a fourth-grade education. Carlos was smart and funny with a knack for getting us in trouble. He quickly became my best friend.

Throughout the fifth grade, no one wore shoes. Our feet were tough as cowhide, so who needed shoes? Starting sixth grade, however, they were required. This was to prepare us for the real world, I suppose. I had only one pair—ankle boots—and the right one was missing a heel. Eventually, I pried off the other heel and threw it away because I got tired of walking with a limp.

During the summer months, Carlos and I fished every chance we got. The Rio Pesqueria flowed through Los Ramones, and there were a number of good fishing holes up and down the river. Fishing was very important to me. It put fresh food on our table, and it allowed me to get away from my always-oppressive family life.

Carlos and I used several different fishing techniques. One was line fishing with regular old cane poles. First, though, we had to catch our bait. We had tiny hooks, which I had bought in the States; and with a tortilla and a hook, we could catch enough minnows to go for the bigger fish.

We would each get a three-foot cane pole and about four feet of thread and tie a hook on the end. Then we would bite a tiny piece of a tortilla off—just enough to fit on the tip of the hook—and dangle it in the water; and in a flash, a minnow would bite! It was similar to catching bigger fish except you had to be a lot faster. Fierce concentration and lightening-speed reflexes were required. Those little buggers were fast and could pick a hook clean in a blur. We usually turned this into a game to see who could catch the most minnows in the shortest length of time. When we'd catch twenty or so minnows, we would go into deeper water and begin fishing in earnest.

Another fishing technique we used was *cueveando* (caving), which in English is called "noodling." It was the only way to catch fish in the summer months because the pools were fairly shallow; and when the water gets warm, catfish hide in caves and holes under rocks at the bottom to stay cool. You can't entice them with bait.

Caving requires steely nerves and lung power. I would take a deep breath, hold it, and dive under water, feeling along the bottom until I found a rock. Then I would search for openings beneath it. I had to be very careful not to spook the fish if they were hiding there. Once I found an opening, I'd come up for air, then dive again, block whatever openings I could with one hand, and reach under the rock with the other. If I was lucky, there was a fish there; and if I could work my hand around the fish's head, I could wriggle him out of his hiding place. Once, I got my hand caught under a huge rock and couldn't get free. As I frantically tried to work myself loose, I started running out of air and began panicking. Eventually, I pulled my soon-to-be bleeding hand out—just in time to surface and take huge gulps of delicious air.

Sometimes there were things under those rocks other than catfish. Once one of my buddies pulled out what he thought was a handful of *mojarras* (bluegills). Instead, it was a huge water snake. We were right next to each other; and when we saw the snake, we both yelled in terror and practically flew out of that pool. The snake, unperturbed, went on with his business.

Some days, we would grab some salt and a half kilo of tortillas at the tortilla factory and cook our own catch. And since we never went anywhere without our slingshots, on the days when our aim was good, we'd shoot frogs, rabbits, doves and other birds and cook them on the spot, too. If you're from the south, look out your window. If you see birds of any size, I've probably eaten them. I once shot a buzzard with a sling shot, but we didn't eat it. It was too nasty.

One morning, Carlos came by and asked if I could go fishing with him. I was eleven years old at the time. I asked Dad, who was reading his Bible, and he gave me the OK. So I asked if we could take the family bicycle. He agreed.

Carlos went home to get his fishing gear. While I waited for him, my younger sister Martha was riding around on the bike. Martha is deaf and to this day, cannot speak. I'm sure she didn't know Dad had given me permission to use the bike.

When Carlos returned, I took the bike from her. I wasn't diplomatic—I just took it. She fought me for it; and when I finally wrestled it from her grip, she hollered and threw herself on the ground, pretending she was having a fit. She did this often—the entire family had seen her do it many times—and everyone knew she was faking it. I'm pretty sure Dad had seen her do it a few times before, so I didn't give it a second thought.

Martha, by the way, was a crucial part of my childhood. Because of her disability, we couldn't put her in school in the United States. In the 1960s, there weren't special facilities like there are now where someone who is deaf can attend school, learn sign language, and otherwise live a normal life. In those days, they had to be sent off to a special school full of all kinds of handicapped children—some mentally disabled.

Martha wasn't mentally disabled; she was 98 percent deaf, and Dad refused to send her off. As it turns out, that was one reason we moved to Mexico—truancy laws were nonexistent there. Even in Mexico, we tried to put her in school once. She couldn't understand the concept of "private property."

Martha was also the reason we went from church to church throughout my childhood, trying to get her healed. I remember going to Pentecostal, Mennonite,

Assembly of God, and other faith-healing churches, and they would promise they could heal her. No one ever did.

So Martha was very protected during our childhood, and I'm sure that explains what happened next.

I went into the kitchen to get some tortillas, and Dad came bursting in. He was furious. "THERE *you* ARE!" he roared. He strode over to me and dropped me with a right cross to the jaw. When I went down, he kicked me around the floor for some time, still yelling. When he finally stopped, he left me there on the dirt floor…bloody…and gasping for air.

I didn't go fishing that day, and that was the last time Dad ever hit me.

Some years later, he wanted to talk about it. He said, "I thought you were a man."

14

The Visionary

S oon after that incident, Dad decided he needed to fast and pray. He fasted for five days and nights with no food or water. I saw him go out to a tree branch in the backyard every morning and do pull-ups. He could still do them on day three. After that, he was too weak.

His fasting was very fruitful. He started having dreams—important dreams. In many of them, he received inspiration about the nature of God, and the most important revelation he had was that God is Love. Those of us who have studied the Bible have read those words, but he saw them in a whole new light. Not only is God love, but there is nothing unloving about God.

If it isn't love, it isn't God. Dad began dissecting the Bible and looking at the Scriptures that portrayed God as violent, jealous, or vengeful. He came to believe that those Scriptures portrayed a false image of God, skewed through the eyes of men, and that Jesus came to dispel that image and show us God's true nature.

Dad began teaching that God is love and that Jesus was blameless and died for our sins. He further clarified that the Bible is not the Word of God. Rather, it is a book that *contains* the Word of God. He taught that Jesus is God Incarnate, and the life and words of Jesus are the true Word of God.

It was during this time that Dad quit teaching the Pauline epistles altogether. He had always had his issues with Paul, but here he saw even more differences between the God of Paul and the God of Jesus. His contention was that Paul was an impostor and didn't really know Jesus and still taught the old God. He was very concerned that Paul turned people over to Satan "for the destruction of their flesh." He would state that Jesus would never partner up with Satan for anything.

He pointed out that Jesus taught us to love our enemies, "That ye may be the children of your Father which is in heaven: for he makes his sun to rise on the evil and on the good, and sends rain on the just and on the unjust." Paul taught, "Pray for your enemies, for in doing so, ye shall heap coals of fire upon their heads" Not exactly a message of love.

All this was very inspiring to me. I would sit in Dad's services and listen to what he had to say. I was very happy for the good news he preached, but then I would look at Dad's actions, and the two didn't mesh.

Even at age eleven, I believed Dad had a very violent nature, and he would only be able to carry his message so far. He had been steeped in violence, and like King David in the Old Testament, he had too much "blood on his hands" to "build God's Temple." King David was one of God's most cherished servants, but when he offered to build Yahweh's Temple, Yahweh declined. Instead, he told David he would bear a son, Solomon, who would be a peaceful man, and God would provide a time of peace to the Israelites, and Solomon would build the Temple in Jerusalem.

I, therefore, saw myself as the one who would "build God's temple." And yet, I knew that I, too, had been steeped in violence—perhaps to a lesser extent than Dad, but violence nevertheless, and would only be able to take it so far before turning it over to someone yet more peaceful than I.

In Dad's dreams, he also received teachings about the "intention of the heart." He rejected the teaching so popular today that all you have to do is get on your knees and "mumble a few magic words" and you'll be saved forever. He asserted that God forgives us for our sins an unlimited number of times as long as our intentions are good, we regularly confess our sins and ask forgiveness, and are not giving ourselves permission to live a sinful life. He would say, "It doesn't matter how many times you fall down; what matters is that you get back up and keep walking toward Jesus." But he also taught that it is possible for a person to "turn away from God" and lose his or her salvation.

Spiritually, Dad divided people into three categories: those who had not received Jesus, those who had but were young in Christ and weak and fell often, and those who were mature and didn't practice sin on a regular basis.

The first category he invited to the communion table. This was his "altar call," if you will. If a person was ready to walk that walk and turn his will and life over to God, Dad invited him to declare his "intention to trust and follow Jesus." Those who were mature he invited to give Jesus the marriage vows.

At the age of eleven, I declared my marriage vows to Jesus, "My Lord Jesus, I promise to love, honor, and obey You, in sickness or in health, in richness or poorness, living or dying, and to be subject to You in all things even unto death."

This was a time of great growth for me. Although I saw Dad as violent and proud and arrogant, I could also see his intentions were good, and I could see the power of his teachings and felt I was on the right path. I envisioned myself bringing thousands of people to this great truth: that God is, indeed, Love, and Jesus is Love Incarnate. I could look to Jesus for my example; and I could look to Mom, as well. I had never seen Mom say an unkind word about anyone; and although Dad talked about love, Mom *was* love. Mom was my real teacher.

So my childhood was marked by a dilemma. On the one hand, I had seen a mighty vision, if you will, which set the course for my entire life. On the other, my eyes were opened. I could see Dad's nature and everything that was wrong about him through the teachings that he himself taught.

I was torn.

And, of course, I saw my own faults almost not at all.

15

Getting Whupped

I had my share of fights growing up in Mexico. I'm sure I had a part in starting some of them, but they were usually not entirely my fault. After all, I was the only white kid in my class.

One day while coming home from school, I was waylaid by this kid I knew as Beto el de Lina. I don't remember what started it; but he hit me, got me in a headlock, wrestled me to the ground, and started punching me in the face. Ground and pound they call it these days. I was defenseless.

I'm not sure what ended the onslaught, but eventually he let me up. Maybe he just got bored. I was beaten and battered, my school clothes were filthy and torn, my books were scattered all over the dusty street, and my left eye was rapidly swelling shut. On wobbly legs, I finished the trek home, adrenaline coursing through my veins.

Dad asked the inevitable question, "Son, did you turn the other cheek?"

"Yes!" I said.

"Did you fight back?"

"No!" which was strictly true. I hadn't fought back—not because I was some kind of a saint, but because Beto was much bigger and had completely overpowered me. Plus, I was a coward.

Dad got very angry and demanded to know who had beaten me. I told him; and soon I was being paraded down the street towards Beto's house so Dad could give Lina, Beto's mother, a piece of his mind. An entourage of gawkers and onlookers trailed along—a symphony of bare feet slapping the dusty road behind me.

We marched past Don Joaquin's house (where Carlos and I stole fruit from the peach trees at night, and if they were still green, we'd sprinkle them with salt and eat them anyway), around the corner past Srta. Adela's adobe shack (she was my sixth grade teacher, a formidable woman—all of five feet tall—who terrorized my scalp daily with *coscorrones*, sharp raps of her knuckles, aided by a huge gold ring, which she dispensed freely to students in her classroom), past the central square where dozens of people were always congregating, and through Lina's front door.

Lina was the local nurse; and she was somewhat frightened when my raving lunatic father barged angrily into her house, yelling in broken Spanish, and dragging his battered urchin in tow. He presented me as a paragon of Christian virtue while Beto was some kind of monster.

I knew what I was.

We left, the screen door slamming behind us. I tentatively followed Dad as he proudly strode back home. I was thoroughly discredited in front of the whole town, my reputation as a coward etched in stone. Not only could I not take a whupping, my daddy had to intervene. I vowed I would never lose a fight again.

Six months later, Beto died.

He suffocated himself with his own pillow during an epileptic seizure.

16

My Little Turtle

One day, I was fishing in a stock tank, and right beside me in about an inch of water was a newly hatched turtle with the eggshell still on its back. It was the cutest little thing—a little over an inch in diameter—and of course, I had to take it home.

I made a home for him in a shoebox and put rocks and dirt in it with a bowl of water. I reasoned he was a snapping turtle, given where I found him, so I knew he would need a watery home.

Dad had made a dining table out of cinder blocks and boards; and that was where we studied; so every afternoon after school, I would come home, get the turtle out of his box, and sit down at the table to do my homework.

Usually, that involved Gregg Shorthand. We were required to take it because Professor Jesus knew shorthand; and since he was one of four teachers who lived in Monterrey and came up for the week to teach us, it was a part of our core curriculum.

Shorthand homework was particularly boring because it consisted of endlessly drawing the symbols on notebook paper. Each day, Professor Jesus assigned us five words for homework; and we had to do five pages of each word in Gregg shorthand; so if one of the words was *palabra*, I would have to write it in shorthand over and over and over again.

Sometimes I would get so bored writing the same symbol over and over that I would get three pencils and hold them so that each pencil lined up with a line on the paper, and *presto!* I could do three lines of symbols at the same time. This was a quicker way of getting homework done, but it was still hopelessly monotonous.

It was much more fun playing with my little turtle.

So I would put him on my notebook as I was doing my homework and watch him walk slowly across the page, and I would write, *Palabra. Palabra. Palabra.*

Maybe he's hungry, I wondered. *What does he eat?* So then I would start looking around for something he might like. I went to the kitchen, got a tortilla, and tried giving him little pieces of it, but he wasn't even slightly interested. He would slowly work his way across my notebook, and I'd drop little chunks right in front of him. Not only would he ignore them, but he would walk right over them like they didn't even exist!

He didn't like beans, either.

Palabra. Palabra. Palabra....
Palabra. Palabra. Palabra....
Palabra. Palabra. Palabra....

So I thought, *I wonder what he eats in the wild.* And I really had no idea, but I was sure it wasn't cooked people food.

Palabra. Palabra. Palabra....
Palabra. Palabra. Palabra....
Palabra. Palabra. Palabra....

Then I spotted a fly. It was sitting on the table right next to my notebook. I inched my open, slightly cupped hand ever so slowly toward the fly; and when my hand was about six inches away, *whoosh!* I tried to grab it!

When I cautiously opened my hand to see if I had caught it, it flew away.

Rats!

Gotta get this homework done!

Palabra. Palabra. Palabra....
Palabra. Palabra. Palabra....
Palabra. Palabra. Palabra....

I wonder what'll happen if I squeeze the fly after I catch it, even if I don't know that I've caught it. That way, if I do catch it, it can't fly away.

I spotted another fly that had landed on the table and inched my hand up slowly, closer and closer, and tried to grab it.

Whoosh!

I wasn't sure if I had caught it or not, so I squeezed my hand really tight and rolled my fingers around and slowly opened my hand.

There lay a dead fly.

Yuk.

I dropped the fly in front of the turtle as he walked across the page of my notebook. He didn't even notice it. In fact, he walked right over it.

Oh, *jeez....*

Palabra. Palabra. Palabra....
Palabra. Palabra. Palabra....
Palabra. Palabra. Palabra....

Maybe this time, I'll only squeeze it enough to keep it from being able to fly away when I open my hand. That might work.

The next fly that landed on the table got my full attention. I slowly stalked it and *whoosh!* grabbed at it and then ground my fingers in my palm just a little bit before slowly opened my hand. There was the fly! It was trying to fly away, but one of its little wings was damaged.

I dropped it about six inches in front of the little turtle. It started spinning around and around because it was trying to fly with one wing.

My little turtle spotted it and worked those little turtle legs as fast as he could. He covered the six inches to the fly in record turtle time and snapped that little fly right up! Down the hatch it went.

Awesome!

Palabra. Palabra. Palabra.

I wondered how many flies he could eat. Well, he ate three or four flies before he lost interest.

I really *liked* that turtle.

One day, I came home from school and my little turtle was gone. I wasn't sure where he was, but he definitely was not in the box. He wasn't around the box, either. In fact, he was nowhere to be seen.

I looked everywhere for him and finally decided the cat must have pounced on him and ate him...or something.

I was not happy.

Every day thereafter, I came home from school, sat at the table to do my homework, and missed my little turtle. Day after day went by, and I kept doing my shorthand.

I slowly forgot about my turtle.

About two weeks later, as I was sitting at the table doing my homework, my little turtle walked out of a pile of dirty clothes and started across the floor.

Turtle! You're *back!*

17

Savoring Joy

L os Ramones is located in the northeastern part of
Mexico, a semiarid land crisscrossed with deep,
dry *arroyos* (creeks), the surface earth often
scorched and barren of any vegetation. It is common to
find spear– and arrowheads and occasionally ax heads
made of flint lying in plain sight, their wooden handles
long wasted away by the elements.

Despite these harsh conditions, a surprising variety
of plant life can survive in this landscape. The Mesquite
tree produces an edible bean. The seeds in the bean are
too hard to chew and swallow; but you can chew the ripe
bean pods, swallow the juice, and spit out the pulp.

You will also find huisache, yaupon (which if used as roasting wood, will produce diarrhea in those who eat the food—much to a tenderfoot's consternation), and Joshua trees. Texas ebony provides a nutty-flavored seed called a *maguacata* that is harvested, boiled, and peeled when the pods are green.

An assortment of cacti dots this land. Prickly pear produces an edible cactus "tuna" with course, hard seeds. Cholla has spines so sharp and strong they can pierce stout leather boots. Columnar produces a delicious, rich purple fruit called a *pitaya* filled with tiny black seeds known (to the delight of squealing children) for turning urine purple. You will also see a variety of barrel cacti—including eagle's claw, tamarindo, saguaro, ladyfinger, hedgehog, and horse crippler. And of course, there is chile piquin and lots of tumbleweed.

Nearer to water holes and arroyos, you may see *sabinal* (cypress), *nogal* (pecan), and various other water-loving hardwoods. At first glance, this land appears hot and uninhabitable, but on closer inspection, it teems with snakes, lizards of all kinds, rabbits, many types of doves, quail, jack rabbits, white-tail and mule deer, and coyotes.

When near water, if you are patient, you may spot *brachygastra mellifica* (more commonly known as

Mexican honey wasps) collecting water to mix with wood pulp to help build the colony's nest. The Mexicans call them *abejas*—bees—however, they are not bees at all, but tiny wasps. They produce a relatively thin, very sweet honey. Their nests are usually well hidden. To find one, you have to go to a water source, spot a wasp, watch it take off, and follow it over the countryside as far as you can...and then stop...and wait.

Following a flying insect, of course, is not easy, and you can quickly lose it. But if you're on the flight path and watch carefully, you may spot another wasp and follow it as far as possible until eventually, you begin seeing more of them closer to the ground. Now you are getting close to locating the nest.

Honey wasps' nests are roughly spherical, maybe a foot or two in diameter and built up around tree branches or in dense brush. In order to get one, you have to brave the swarming, stinging insects, saw the limbs off the tree or brush on either side of the nest, and try to keep from falling if you are in a tree as you saw, swat, climb, and swat. This is an experience I know something about.

One day while we were playing in Carlos's backyard, we spotted a honey wasp getting water from a puddle under a dripping faucet. We decided to follow it and didn't have far to go. We noticed several other wasps flying around an Osage orange tree right there in the backyard. Looking around in the thick foliage, we eventually spotted the nest, and Carlos decided to climb up and get it.

He went into the house, put on a pair of pants and a long-sleeve shirt, shoes (which we commonly didn't wear), and a windbreaker. He also put a pair of socks over his hands, and finally, a course, very colorful nylon shopping bag over his head, which he tied at the neck. He could barely see through the mesh, and he looked ridiculous.

By now, several friends had gathered to watch the operation. Amid friendly jeering and catcalls, Carlos climbed the tree armed to the teeth with his mom's butcher knife. We laughed uproariously at the spectacle of my best friend, wasps swarming around him, hacking away at the tree branch with his mama's kitchen knife.

Soon he started yelping in pain between peals of laughter as one of the wasps got inside his makeshift bee bonnet. Several other wasps had discovered that since the shopping bag was resting on top of his head and his hair was pretty short, they didn't need to invade the shopping bag. They just lit on the top of his head and started stinging away right through the mesh!

The more he yelped, the harder we laughed; and the harder we laughed, the harder he laughed till he just about fell out of the tree. But he didn't give up. Eventually, he was able to hack away enough of the branch to break it; and after throwing the knife to the ground, he now held the sawed-off branch in one hand with the nest attached and wasps swarming around him.

We stayed far away from him as he climbed down from the tree and walked toward the kitchen, alternately laughing and yelping each time a new wasp found a chink in his armor. Finally, the confused wasps went back to the tree where the nest had been and left us alone.

We took the nest apart in pieces, savoring bites of its delicious paper honeycomb—sucking the sweet honey out and spitting out the pulp. We ate it like candy. The rest we gave to Doña Chelo, Carlos's mom. She made hot flour tortillas, put a piece of honeycomb on each one, and gave the little ones a sweet treat.

18

Living on Faith

Our time in Los Ramones was a relatively stable period in my childhood. We were in school most of the school year, and we ate relatively well.

We had rented a small, adobe house with dirt floors and a thatched roof about two blocks from the main plaza. There was room enough for two bedrooms, a kitchen complete with a cooking fireplace, and one room where we had church services every night. The cooking fireplace was built in such a way that the hearth was waist high. There was a metal tripod where pots were held for cooking and always an earthen pot full of pintos sitting on the coals. There was also a *comal*—a flat piece of metal, somewhat like a griddle, used for making tortillas. Mom had her Coleman camp stove and a folding oven for it, so we were set. On Saturdays, we washed our clothes with a scrub board and hung them up on a clothesline to dry.

Dad built wooden benches for our church services. We had services every single night of the year while we were in town. We bought twenty-kilo bags of oranges and passed them out at the services. In this way, we persuaded people to attend. None of us had musical instruments, so all hymns were sung *a cappella*.

Dad's Spanish was getting pretty good but not good enough to where he could tell when my friends and I changed the lyrics as we sang the hymns. We made up parallel lyrics to a fair number of songs, and Dad never understood why we couldn't keep a straight face through some of them.

Then Dad would preach. Since he preached every night, I knew his sermons by heart; so to distract myself, I would turn to the Old Testament and read about Abraham, Lot, King David, and the prophets. Some of those stories were interesting. Some were rather shocking—for instance, the story of Lot, the only righteous man in Sodom and Gomorrah.

As I read these stories, I tried to reconcile them with the God of Love that Dad was teaching.

Why did the men of that town want to have sex with other men? Why did Lot, a righteous man, offer his own virgin daughters to them instead? And why were Lot's daughters considered sanctified, even though they got their dad drunk and had sex with him? It seemed to me they should have been a part of the crowd who were destroyed.

Then there was the story of Elisha the prophet who, when coming into a town, was jeered by a dozen or so teenagers making fun of his bald head. He cursed them in the name of the Lord, and two she-bears came out of the woods and killed them. This didn't seem to be a very loving thing for a prophet to do, and certainly not the act of a God of Love.

I was very confused.

On September 5, 1967, a small storm developed into a tropical depression east of the Lesser Antilles. It moved slowly through the islands; on September 7, it became Tropical Storm Beulah.

The next day, Beulah reached hurricane strength while continuing slowly west-northwestward, rapidly intensifying until it reached peak winds of 150 mph just south of Mona Passage. When it passed south of Hispaniola, land interaction and upper-level shear greatly weakened the hurricane to a tropical storm; but as it crossed over the western Caribbean, Beulah again strengthened to a major hurricane.

On September 16, Beulah made landfall as a Category 3 hurricane near Cozumel, Mexico. Weakening slightly as it passed over land, the storm gained new strength once it moved over the Gulf of Mexico, rapidly intensifying to its peak 160-mph winds as a Category 5 storm. In terms of size, Beulah became the third largest hurricane on record at the time.

When Hurricane Beulah made final landfall south of Matamoros, Mexico, on September 20, 1967, it produced Category 3 conditions in Texas. The storm drifted over the state, moving southwestward into Mexico before dissipating.

During the time the storm was growing, Dad became very vocal about our stand of faith. He was attempting to get people to trust in God for everything. When Hurricane Beulah skirted the Yucatan peninsula, it turned north and headed straight for us. We were still in Los Ramones, about fifty miles outside of Monterrey, Nuevo Leon, and fifty miles south of the border.

Dad preached nightly that we should pray the hurricane would veer away from us. For several days, we tracked the coordinates on an hourly basis; and when it looked like we were in the bull's eye, we would pray even harder. Dad contended that if we prayed enough, we would be spared.

For most of the last two days, it looked like Beulah was headed right at us. Then on the last day, it headed north, slamming into the coast of northern Mexico. When it proceeded northwest and circled around in a southwesterly direction, it passed to our west bringing our little town much-needed rain.

This, Dad said, was proof that God answered our prayers.

Maybe He did, but I couldn't help thinking about the absurdity of that week-long ordeal: *Does a God of Love count the prayers of the villagers of every little town along the Texas-Mexico coast, find the one with the least number of prayers, and send a Cat 5 hurricane down their throats?*

I was pretty sure there were people praying up and down the coast that the hurricane would spare them. Furthermore, it seemed to me that if God really answered everyone's prayers, He would have had the hurricane fall apart before hitting the Gulf Coast, or turned it around and directed it back out to sea where it could dissipate without harming anyone.

19

The Garden

One of the things Dad found perplexing during our time in Los Ramones was the fact that, although the Mexican people were hard-working folks and regularly went without basic foods, none of them gardened. Most backyards were full of weeds. Since there was very little water—certainly not enough to maintain a lawn—the townspeople either let weeds grow or kept them down, leaving a bare patch of dirt where the kids could play.

So Dad had this brilliant idea. He decided to plant a garden and show the town folks we ministered to how to bring in much-needed food to their tables.

The next time we were in the United States, we bought seeds for all types of vegetables: squash, cucumbers, watermelons, corn, beans, peas, and peppers of all kinds. And when we returned to Los Ramones, we planted them.

Although there was only enough water pressure to have running water an hour or so in the morning and at night, it was enough to give our garden the moisture it needed to grow. Dad dug irrigation ditches all through it, and we planted sunflowers along the fence lines. And the garden flourished. It looked like paradise!

We also raised a few turkeys, ducks, pigs, and goats, so we occasionally had meat.

Before long, we had more vegetables than we could possibly eat, so rarely did a day go by when Dad didn't send one of us kids to a neighbor's house with a sack full of vegetables. He kept this up for three years straight; and in those three years, not one single neighbor started a garden of their own.

One day, Dad went to Monterrey and came back with a volleyball and net, a soccer ball, baseballs, bats, and gloves.

He hoed up the entire garden and turned it into a playground.

20

When Are We Going Home?

An overarching desire in nearly all my childhood memories was the yearning to go back "home." Home was upstate New York, with trees and food and real whole milk straight from the morning milking (the kind you had to shake hard in the bottle before pouring because if you didn't, you'd get an inch of cream in the top of your glass) and People Who Spoke English. At all times in the back of my mind, wherever we were, was the question: *When are we going home?*

I don't think any of us thought we would be missionaries forever. I somehow thought or wished anyway that this little experiment we were in the middle of would finally end, and we would go back to being normal people. It wasn't fun for me to dress like homeless people, even though we were often homeless, or to live in roadside parks or next to water holes, sleeping behind gas stations, and looking for pop bottles in ditches so we could get a little spending money. I hated looking for food in garbage cans and attempting to make friends with people who were picnicking at roadside parks we inhabited so we could eat their leftovers. Being missionaries was hard work.

Every once in awhile though, we would go back to New York and move into the old schoolhouse that was located on Grandma's farm.

Dad had built out the old country schoolhouse where Grandma had taught when he was a child. It hadn't been used since they built the new elementary school in Nichols, so Dad turned it into a nice home with three bedrooms and a kitchen with a wood stove where Mom could cook.

There was no electricity, but we had kerosene lamps for light, and the stove heated the house. There was also no running water or no inside bathroom, but there was a hand pump out in the front yard and an outhouse out back. Dead winter in Upstate New York is pretty chilly, but we made do.

I was happy when we were there.

A cat we named Mama Cat lived with us in New York. Every time we visited Grandma, she showed up at our door. One year, she had her kittens under my bed, and one of them—Nosey—became my very first pet. I named him that because he had a nice black patch on his nose.

Mama Cat was mostly white with some dark markings. Her ears were rounded and about a half inch shorter than they should have been because of frequent frostbite. She was quite a hunter. Once, she brought a chipmunk and a bird home with her. Both were still alive. I don't know how she pulled that off, but she did.

One year when I was still small, someone gave me a little red tractor with pedals, like a tricycle. I loved that little tractor, but the driveway was gravel, and it was hard to get up any speed. The asphalt road that ran by the old schoolhouse, on the other hand, was ideal for that. I could really go fast on that road.

Dad wasn't big on second chances; but when he saw me out there, he told me to get off and stay off the road. I stayed on the driveway for a while; but the road really was the best place for the little red tractor; so eventually, I pedaled it back out on the asphalt.

Dad bellowed as he came running out of the house. He then grabbed me from my little tractor and wrapped it around the old oak tree that stood beside the driveway. When he finished with it, it was nothing more than a twisted piece of metal.

I never rode that little red tractor into the road again.

I never rode it anywhere.

21

Feeling Normal

We always ate good food when we visited Grandma. One of my favorite places in her house was the kitchen because when we were home from Mexico, we were always hungry, and Grandma was always baking something. She was the mother of ten, and she knew how to bake.

Grandma baked bread every day. After my aunts and uncles grew up, Grandma continued to bake bread for Grandpa and Uncle Paul and whoever else happened to be working the farm and eating at their table. I never saw a loaf of store-bought bread in that house in the twenty years I visited or lived there.

I loved watching Grandma bake bread. She'd get out a huge stainless steel bowl, sift in the flour, mix in the other ingredients, and add yeast. After waiting for the dough to rise, she would knead it and spank it to get the bubbles out. I thought it was hilarious that the bread dough needed spanking. Until I was eleven, I got spanked all the time.

Grandma was always on the cutting edge of nutrition; so when oleomargarine came out and was advertised as a healthy alternative to butter, Grandma listened and began putting margarine on the table. Grandpa was aghast. Since he was a dairy farmer and milked registered Holsteins every morning and night, he wasn't having any of that margarine stuff. He would say, "Margarine is a dirty word in this house!" It turns out Grandpa was right. According to most experts today, butter is now recognized to be healthier than margarine, and it definitely tastes better.

Going home also meant seeing my friend Tom. Tom lived on the next farm, maybe a couple hundred yards up Moore Hill Road. The first time we saw each other, we started throwing rocks at each other. After that, we became fast friends. Tom and his brother John would come over and play with my cousins Robbie and Dickey and me. We loved to play in the haymow and build forts with the hay bales and chase each other around in the barn. One day, John tripped and fell face first in the drop (the concrete trench in the milking barn, strategically placed behind the cow's rear end where manure drops). He had to go home and get cleaned up.

When I was twelve, we finally made a trip back home. We had been gone for three straight years, and I couldn't wait to see Tom. We got in late at night, but I was so excited that I got up really early the next morning to go see him.

I didn't want to awaken his parents, so I found a ladder and climbed through Tom's second-story bedroom window. When I woke him, he sat up in bed and listened, still half asleep, while I excitedly caught him up on my news. When he finally climbed out of bed and stood up, my heart sank.

Tom was a full six inches taller than I was, had a deep voice, and wore sideburns. I still had my squeaky voice and not even a promise of sideburns. I decided our friendship was over. *Why would he want to play with me?* But Tom would have none of that, and soon we were eating pancakes downstairs, ready to go out for some adventure.

One of the things we got to do was help Uncle Jay get his hay in. Uncle Jay was Grandpa's brother and a fine old man. He lived alone on the original piece of land that the Moores had settled in the late 1700s. Uncle Jay had a big, reddish nose and silky, white hair. He always wore coveralls and flannel shirts and chewed Red Man tobacco…and he was always nice to me. I was such a little guy that year when we brought in the hay that he insisted I drive the tractor while he and Tom threw the bales on the wagon. Imagine that! I got to drive the tractor! *It doesn't get any better than this,* I thought to myself.

Later that week, Tom and I were racing bikes down the very steep hill between Tom's and Uncle Jay's farms. After passing the Moore place, the road crosses Varguson's Creek and then goes up a steep hill about a quarter mile away.

Tom's bike had a speedometer on it. I was riding a "banana" bike that belonged to one of my cousins. We would start at the top and pedal downhill as fast as we could until one of us chickened out and hit the brakes. The banana bike didn't have brakes, but that was no problem. When I wanted to stop, I could just haul back on the handlebars, put my sneakers on each side of the front tire, and apply enough pressure to slow the bike to a stop.

Uncle Jay and his neighbor Archie Babcock were standing in Jay's front yard talking, kind of keeping an eye on us, when we went up the hill for what was to be our last race.

We pushed the bikes hard, jumped on them, and pedaled as fast as we could. The speedometer on Tom's bike read 55 mph, and we were keeping up with each other. I figured that was as fast as I wanted to go, so I hauled back on the handlebars and put my sneakers up on the front wheel.

This time instead of the handlebars giving me the leverage to put pressure on the tires, they came loose and rotated down over my knees, trapping my legs and preventing me from controlling the bike. I could barely balance it and certainly couldn't stop, and I didn't think I could make it all the way to the bottom because I was gaining speed. So I decided to ditch the bike as best I could, right in Jay's front yard.

First, though, I had to cross the ditch itself, a two- or three-foot deep affair lined with flat rocks. I hit the ditch hard, flew through the air, landed in the grass, and rolled past Uncle Jay and Archie before coming to a stop.

They were so startled that they just stood there and looked at me. I got up in a daze, dusted myself off, and mumbled I was OK. I left the bicycle where it lay, walked to Grandma's house, and went to bed. For two days.

Whenever we went back home to New York, I had the best time. But inevitably, Dad would load us back up in the Old Truck (or whatever car we currently had) and haul us back down that dreaded road.

22

Moriah

B oy. Such a simple name for a dog. I've always
wondered why I named him that; surely, I could
have come up with a more imaginative name.

Boy came into my life like so many of my pets did: he
was a rescue animal. Mom used to kid me about it.
When we would land somewhere, whether it was a small
village or a watering hole that we called home for awhile,
I would find a stray and wounded animal and bring it
home for her to nurse back to life. Birds with broken
wings, cats so mangy they had little fur, creatures large
and small: I brought them all home to Mom. Mom was
the healer.

The first time I saw Boy, he was being tortured. Some folks have a mean streak, and Boy was the object of gruesome pleasure. His legs were lassoed with three ropes, and he was being pulled apart by a circle of laughing men.

A woman who loved animals shamed those men and stopped the torture and took Boy home with her. Because I wanted a dog, he somehow ended up with me. Mom told me later she and Dad brought Boy home for me so I wouldn't run away.

It is almost impossible to describe the bond that forms between a boy and his dog, especially when they have adventures together, and Boy became my best friend. Whether I was hunting or fishing or playing games with the other kids in town, Boy was always by my side.

About six months after Boy came to live with us, he started having fits. One day, he just went into convulsions and start foaming at the mouth. According to Dad, he had snapped at a little kid during one of those fits, and Dad decided he needed to put Boy down. There was no such thing as a veterinary doctor in our little village, and we didn't have a gun, so Dad decided he had to do it himself. My older brother Dan told me later that

Dad asked him to go with him to help do the dirty work, but Dan refused. He wasn't stupid. I was chosen instead.

We loaded Boy in the car and drove out to a nearby creek. Boy was very happy to be taking a ride out into the country. He loved riding in the car and eagerly jumped in. He was ready for some fun.

We stopped and got out of the car. Boy jumped out of the back seat and began making his rounds, peeing on the bushes, sniffing the air. Dad got an ax, a hunting knife, and a piece of rope out of the car, and we began walking. Dad was looking for exactly the right spot.

We soon came upon a place where water had washed under the fence row, leaving a ledge about two feet high right next to a post. A perfect altar for what was to come. Although Boy became pretty alarmed at what was going on, he allowed Dad to tie him up to the fence post. Dad tied him up so tight against the ledge that Boy couldn't move his head. Then Dad raised the ax and hit him as hard as he could. He must have thought he could kill that dog with one blow, but it didn't happen that way. Boy let out a scream that sounded like nothing I'd ever heard in my life. It had every emotion man or animal had ever known.

Then Dad hit him again. And again.

I couldn't believe what I was seeing. I kept thinking: *Dad! Stop! Can't we just call this off?* I thought about trying to stop him myself. *Dad would listen, wouldn't he? Dad was always right, wasn't he? Dad loved dogs, didn't he?* But I was more terrified of Dad and I couldn't make myself move to save Boy. I was frozen.

As Dad kept raining blows down on Boy's head, the dog kept roaring; and all the while, he was looking straight at me, begging me, wanting me to do something to stop the carnage; but I couldn't move. I realized that even if Dad stopped, Boy would never be okay. I could never put him back together again. There was no turning back. Dad had to finish it. Boy had to die. Now, I just wished it was over.

Boy's head was mutilated, but he was still very much alive. Dad started crying in frustration, and then he began bellowing. This wasn't going as planned; Boy was a tough dog, far from dead. He was still roaring, a deep, guttural scream escaping from his blood-foam, broken mouth.

By now, Dad was sobbing. He clearly didn't know what to do next. He pulled out his hunting knife and started stabbing Boy in the chest, thrusting the blade between Boy's ribs where his heart was and moving the handle back and forth, back and forth, trying to shred it.

He stabbed him and stabbed him again and again. The dog still wouldn't die. I was petrified.

Finally after what seemed an eternity, the carnage was over. Dad, still sobbing with frustration and anger, went to the car and got the old folding Army shovel and began digging a big hole. Angrily cursing and sweating profusely, he buried Boy's mutilated body.

I wanted to run away, but I didn't have anywhere to go, and we were miles from town.

We got in the car and drove back home. I don't remember much after that.

I had betrayed my best friend.

23

Althea
Makes a Break for It

Romance in small town Mexico is interesting. In a typical village, there is a town square, called *la Plaza*. In the middle of the plaza is a raised kiosk. In our town, it was simply called *el Kiosko*. In most villages, the kiosko has a few park benches inside it. If there is an event that requires a public speech, it is delivered from the kiosko.

Around most village kioskos is a paved sidewalk, ten or twelve feet wide—wide enough for three or four girls to walk side by side, around and around.

Separated from this sidewalk by four or five feet of grass is another sidewalk—again circling the kiosko, again ten or twelve feet wide—wide enough for three or four guys to walk around and around, side by side.

Surrounding the whole plaza is the main sidewalk, usually flanked by trees of various kinds with park benches underneath. Streets frame the plaza, and across the streets you will often find the municipal building, a Catholic church, at least five *cantinas* (beer joints), a few cafes, and the homes of various more well-to-do residents of the town.

On a typical weekend night on the main sidewalk, you will discover *paleta* carts, little stores offering sweets, sodas and beer, trinkets and toys, cigarettes, clothing, and other items. You will see parents gossiping with each other, drinking and eating, and keeping an eye on their children who are busy playing whatever game is in season.

While the parents are keeping one eye on the kids, the other eye is tracking the courting that is occurring on the two inner sidewalks of the plaza. On the first sidewalk, young men are walking clockwise, talking, laughing, and showing off. Each time they make a trip around, they get a chance to check out each and every young woman who is walking counterclockwise on the sidewalk closest to the kiosko. This allows all the young men in the village to check out all the young women in the village many times during a typical evening, and vice versa.

If a guy sees a girl he likes, he will try to make eye contact with her. If she likes him, eventually she will make eye contact with him. He will then make a side comment to his buddies, who will laugh. In response, she may smile or giggle a bit and say something to her friends who are walking with her. The tension mounts.

During the next several go-arounds, the guy may get up the nerve to speak to the girl. This is a time of great pressure, for everyone is keenly aware of who is watching whom. If he speaks to her and she likes him, she may reply. Or she may ignore him for awhile until he gets up the nerve to speak to her again on the next go-around. If the girl doesn't like him, she will find a way to let him know. Of course, guys being guys, he may keep making advances even though she is clearly rejecting him. He must do this because his reputation is on the line. If she doesn't like him and rejects him, he must save face somehow. Maybe he'll tell his buddies that he doesn't really like her. After all, there's another girl he has been flirting with as they walk 'round and 'round. He can't simply look beaten down. If at all possible, he must look as if whatever happens is the outcome he wanted all along.

For the young lady's part, if she likes the guy, she must not appear to like him too much. She may show modest interest, but she mustn't encourage him too openly because her reputation is at stake. This is noted by her parents; and as they keep an eye on her, she is observing them as well. She wants to see how they are reacting to her interest in the young man. If she sees they are reacting somewhat favorably to his advances, on the next go-around if he speaks to her again, she may smile or reply.

Around again they go.

When the suitor is pretty clear his maiden of choice is interested in talking with him, on the next go-around, he will speak to her again, and she will stop to reply. They might step off the sidewalk to the grass between walkways so as to not interrupt the other walkers. This first encounter may last thirty seconds or ten minutes. There will be no physical contact at this point in time.

If all goes well, the very nervous and excited couple may go sit on a park bench together and talk, always aware of the watchful eyes of her parents. Under no circumstances are they allowed to go outside the plaza or across the street. They must stay in the plaza in full view of her parents. If their first conversation is promising, they may begin to meet on a regular basis, every weekend night in front of everyone, in the open, in the plaza.

If this courtship continues, at some point the young man will make an appointment with the young woman's parents, and he will ask them for her hand in marriage. Under no circumstances will he propose to her before taking this step. If they accept, both sets of parents will meet. Usually in a small town, they have known each other all their lives. Together, the parents of the young couple will plan the wedding and the reception. Typically, the parents of the bride will pay for most of the expenses.

The entire village will be invited to the reception. No one waits for an invitation. It is understood that unless you are one of the beggars of the town (and every town has at least one beggar family) or you share a deep enmity with one or both sets of parents, you are invited.

A pit is dug the night before at the location where the reception will take place, and a huge mesquite fire is lit. The coals of the fire are dumped into the bottom of the pit and covered with wet burlap. Onto that, a skinned head of a cow, also wrapped in wet burlap, is lowered. This is covered with more wet burlap, followed by stones or bricks. The cow head cooks slowly all night long. In the morning, the cow head is dug up and the meat is carefully picked off the head and served to the wedding guests with tortillas, side dishes, sodas, and beer. This is called *barbacoa*.

The couple is married in the Catholic church that morning, and they join the reception afterward. Gifts are given, and pacts between families are made. The wedding and reception are followed by a dance that lasts long into the evening. Usually, there is no honeymoon. The couple quietly leaves the reception, goes to their prepared house, and consummates their marriage.

There may be huge variations to this scenario, however. If the parents are poor and cannot afford a wedding, or if either set of parents disapproves of the engagement and the couple insists on getting married anyway, then another arrangement must be made: the couple must elope.

Here's how it is done.

The couple picks a respected married couple in the community, usually an older couple who approves of their desire to be married. The couple agrees to meet at a certain time and place and from there go together to the home of the respected couple. The young woman stays there, while the young man goes to the police station. There he tells the justice of the peace he has eloped with the young woman. The word he uses is *raptada* (raptured). The young man is then voluntarily incarcerated.

The justice of the peace sends a deputy to the home of the young woman's parents. The deputy explains to them that their daughter has been raptada and is in a safe place. "*Se la robo* (he stole her)," the deputy says. He tells them the young man has turned himself in and is in custody, and he asks the parents if they will give their permission for the couple to marry.

If they grant permission, the young man is released from jail.

After some hemming and hawing, the young woman's parents usually consent, and the couple marries privately without a reception and *baile* (dance). If the parents are poor, they have saved face. If the parents disapprove of the marriage, they have washed their hands of it and are not responsible if it fails.

Usually, everyone eventually accepts the marriage, and they all get along. The sponsor couple typically becomes godparents of the firstborn from the union.

⸻⟡⸻

My nickname in Los Ramones was *Cuñado*, which means brother-in-law. This was because I had three sisters, and the loftiest goal of every Mexican man was to marry an American woman, paving the way for legal entry into the United States. The poverty in those villages was so brutal and work so scarce that in the spring, most of the men would head illegally to the good ol' USA. They would chase the crops being harvested across the country and return in late fall in their shiny new trucks to be with their families.

If they married an American girl, their troubles were over. They no longer had to cross illegally; they could work more hours and get better jobs; they could even take their families on the road with them and not miss them so much. So I was Cuñado.

One afternoon when I was thirteen years old, *El Comandante*, (the deputy) came by our house. He wanted to talk to Dad.

Dad came out to the backyard. He knew something was up because Althea had been missing for several hours, and no one had been able to find her.

The deputy explained to Dad that his daughter had been raptada, and the man responsible was in the county jail.

Dad, of course, was very upset. His Spanish was not as good as ours; and when he heard the word *raptada*, he thought it meant raped. Althea was fifteen years old.

Dad understood why the young man was in jail. What he didn't get was why they wanted Dad to let him out. And he didn't yet understand that she had eloped, wanted to get married, and was gone for good.

Eventually, he consented, and Althea was married shortly thereafter.

I'm ashamed to say I mostly sided with Dad. I thought she was too young to marry; but I was happy that for once, I was not the object of His wrath. And secretly, I admired her for getting out.

Dan left shortly thereafter.

I was now the oldest child in the household.

24

Más Escuela

I was in the third-ever ninth grade class in Los Ramones. My grades were excellent, and my mastery of Spanish was complete. I was spending a lot of time running the streets, getting into trouble, and becoming a little too cocky and confident.

Although I had straight As in school, I was lazy. I hated school with all its rules and regulations. I disliked wearing the school uniform with khaki pants, white shirt, and black clip-on tie during the hottest days of the school year. There was no such thing as air conditioning, and the temperature regularly got into the hundreds. Dan had graduated, Althea had eloped, and I was now in the highest grade in the Mexican school system before college. School in Mexico extended only nine grades, so I had entered seventh grade as a sophomore.

The school day was divided into two segments. Morning classes started at eight o'clock and ended at eleven thirty when we broke for lunch and *siesta*. Afternoon classes resumed at two o'clock and ended at four thirty. All the important classes—biology, history, civics, physics, and Spanish—were held in the morning. The rest—English, shop, sports, band, and Gregg Shorthand—were held in the afternoon, largely because many students gave into the temptation to skip the afternoon session and go fishing.

I enjoyed certain autonomy in high school. I was now taller than most of my classmates; and although I was pretty skinny, I wasn't picked on as much. And because I got straight As in my coursework, I didn't get hassled much by the teachers.

I decided one day that in order to avoid studying completely, all I needed to do was steal the tests to get the grades I wanted. After the first quarter, however, my plan backfired. I had a hard time keeping my mouth shut, and I bragged about stealing the exams. Some of the other students decided to take the easy way, too. Pretty soon, all the copies of the tests in the teachers' desks were gone. This was before computers, so assessments needed to be banged out on a typewriter and then mimeographed, and since the nearest mimeograph machine was in Monterrey—fifty miles away—the teachers had to start from scratch to create a whole new set of exams.

This was only a minor setback for me. I had a system for getting good grades between exams. I knew my friend Olivia studied each and every night. Before school, I would approach her on the playground to ask what each class was about, and she would narrate what she learned from homework the night before. As soon as I got into that particular class, I would scan the material and get familiar with it. In five or ten minutes, I was up to speed and ready to present the oral exam. Since half of our grade was oral, I'd make sure I knew the material the first few days of the quarter; then when the teacher asked questions, my hand would shoot up. When I got called on to "give the class," I got a grade, so then I didn't have to study for the rest of the quarter. To look good, I would raise my hand even when I knew the teachers wouldn't call on me. In this way, I became the teachers' pet.

I particularly excelled in the sciences—physics, chemistry, and biology. I disliked history, however, especially when they covered the Mexico–Texas War. History classes in Mexico taught that Texas, New Mexico, Arizona, and California belonged to Mexico, and the United States took those states away. Since I was an American, when it came time to study this section, some of my classmates would become belligerent towards me and want to fight. I would always tell them I had nothing to do with it.

There were three grades in Escuela Secundaria Don Benito Juarez: seventh, eighth, and ninth; and we had four professors who came in from Monterrey on Monday, stayed the week teaching, and then left on the bus on Friday. Professor Melchor was the principal, Professor Jesus was the vice principal, and there were two other teachers at different times.

Occasionally, the river would rise enough during a rainy period so the teachers could not make it across the bridge. Then classes would be canceled. I made note of this; and one Monday, Carlos, Gerardo, and I stood at the entrance gate and told the students as they arrived that there were no classes because the teachers hadn't been able to come.

They thanked us, turned around, and went home. There was no school that day. The next day, of course, we were in trouble; but since all three of us made good grades and Carlos was the acting mayor's son, our punishment was minimal. I don't think the teachers minded a day off, anyway.

25

Dreamer of Dreams

One day as I walked into the house after school, Dad said, "Get your stuff together. We're leaving." He then continued talking to Mom about a dream he had the night before and what it meant. This was a common thing: Dad waking up and announcing his dreams to us and telling us how he interpreted them. I would just roll my eyes.

This time, I was pissed off. It seemed to me that even though I hated being in Mexico and wanted to "go home" to Grandma's house, Los Ramones had, at the very least, become my home away from home. I was pretty close to Carlos, had a few other friends, and enjoyed myself at school.

We were packed and gone by nightfall. We told no one we were leaving or when or if we were coming back. I didn't even get to say goodbye to Carlos.

We were headed south.

Crammed into the front seat of an old, green 1956 Buick Special (our vehicle at the time) were Dad, Mom, Ruth, and me. Martha, the youngest, was lying on the plywood ledge that went from the back of the front seat to the back window ledge. Under the ledge, in the trunk, and strapped to the roof was everything we owned. There was no arguing with Dad; so I just swallowed my fury and rode in silence, the passenger door handle jammed in my side.

Many years later, I received a form of physical therapy called Rolfing. This is a deep-tissue therapy, much deeper than massage, designed to release emotional energy from the body. When my therapist got to my right side where that door handle had been jammed that night, I burst into tears, and the images of that night came flooding back to me.

We drove south, day after day, deeper into Mexico than we had ever been. The regional food changed as we went into the tropics. Corn husk tamales gave way to banana leaf tamales. Pinto beans gave way to black beans. We stayed in city parks by night, sleeping at the curb of the plazas. Dad had welded a frame made of angle iron to the top of the car and built a wooden shelf on it so that he and I—the "men"—could sleep on top at night, covered with a tarp to keep us from getting wet with dew, while the "women" slept sitting inside the car.

I had kept my textbooks; and during the day, I read as much as I could. I was so angry that I dared not speak to Dad. My responses were yes and no. He droned on and on to Mom about his latest dream and what it meant. I wasn't interested in his dreams any longer, the excitement of my own vision a long-faded memory.

As we neared the southern border of Mexico in the state of Chiapas, the mountains started getting pretty steep. We were working our way up the Sierra Madre del Sur. The scenery was spectacular with coffee *fincas* growing up very steep inclines and corn fields planted at seemingly impossible angles. I, however, was not in the frame of mind to appreciate any of it. The car was so overloaded, I would joke that it looked like a frog with signs on its sides. With all that extra weight, the engine regularly overheated. Dad's response was to turn on the heater full blast to help dissipate some of the heat off the engine; so not only were we hot from being in the tropics, but now we had the heater blowing on us full blast. I was miserable and spent much of my time scheming and dreaming of getting away once and for all from my father, who I thought was a mad man.

After five or six days on the road, we came to the Guatemalan border.

I thought Mexico was poor. Guatemala was poor at an entirely new level. As we worked our way through difficult mountain passes, we at times encountered places where half of the road had been washed into gullies hundreds, even thousands of feet below. The local Indians wore *traje*—the traditional Highland Mayan costume. I saw very few women, but the men wore what looked like plaid skirts and in some cases headwear. In my mind, their skirts resembled kilts.

In spite of my anger, I was fascinated by the Mayan culture. We went through places with exotic names like Quetzaltenango and Chichicastenango. When we got high enough into the mountains, the rarefied air was cool, and it seemed there were active volcanoes everywhere with huge plumes of steam coming out of the mountainsides right next to the road.

We came to rest at Lago de Atitlán, a clear, cold body of water in the highlands of Guatemala. This lake is surrounded by three large volcanoes: Volcán Tolimán, Volcán Atitlán, and Volcán San Pedro. It seemed to me I was always looking straight up at the peak of one of them and their plumes of smoke rising from the top.

We sat there for three weeks in a national park. During that time, I became friends with quite a few of the kids who came over to fish every day from the local village. No one went to school—even kids as young as eight came to fish. I asked them why they weren't in school. They said no one they knew went to school—they had to go out every day and find food for their families. Whereas in Mexico, people would throw back the smaller fish they caught, in Guatemala, they kept every fish, no matter how small.

I recall with fondness one very cool morning, high in the mountains, when we stopped at a local market to buy something for breakfast. We were offered a hot sweet drink called *horchata*. It warmed me to the bone, and it was one of the most delicious things I had ever tasted. It was made with rice, sugar, and coconut milk, and it came with a curled piece of cinnamon bark for stirring.

After a few weeks, Dad decided to head east to Puerto Barrios, a seaport on the eastern shore of that tiny country. We began our descent from the volcanic peaks where the air was cool and crisp. Within a span of twenty-six miles, we arrived in a steaming jungle.

The heat and humidity were oppressive. I always thought I could easily live in the tropics as long as I was living at a high altitude. I didn't like the jungle with its dense vegetation, loud monkeys and birds, snakes, and mosquitoes.

Guatemala was in the middle of a low-grade civil uprising; so when we showed up with a car painted with signs on both sides and the back and a huge loudspeaker mounted on the roof, we got a bit too much unwanted attention from soldiers who would stop us and demand to see our papers. There were a few tense moments when they examined our visas, trying to decide if we were insurgents or not. Usually, a few dollars spread among them eased their moods.

As we entered Puerto Barrios, I was disgusted by the sewage system. There were canals running through many of the poor areas, and outhouses were built on poles that spanned the canals. Raw sewage just dropped straight down into the black water below. It was appalling.

We left Guatemala after about a month and headed north once again, with Dad still trying to interpret his nightly dreams. As we crossed the border back into Mexico, we met four college students from the Universidad de Guatemala. They were an exuberant lot, driving a brand new Volkswagen bug and on vacation, headed for a grand adventure in Mexico City. They were ahead of us as we went through customs, so they were on their way while we were still getting searched.

We soon caught up with them, however. They were broke down by the side of the road with a flat tire. They had no tools and nothing to change the tire with, so we stopped to help them. Dad patched their inner tube, and off they went.

After a few miles, we caught up with them again. They were beside the road with another flat. I think we changed a total of three tires for them. Apparently, the inner tubes made in Guatemala were fabricated with defective rubber; and as soon as the tires got hot, the rubber disintegrated. I enjoyed helping them; although, I hated to see their excitement die just a little bit with each flat tire.

We drove for a day or so and stopped at a small city in the state of Veracruz called Tres Valles. The town was nestled in the lowland mountains with jungle all around it. Pico de Orizaba, the third tallest peak in North America, was about a hundred miles away and clearly visible in the morning air. Dad decided we were going to stay awhile.

We rented a small house that had been built under a mango grove. The walls were made of boards, and between each board was a gap about an inch wide. It was designed this way so air could circulate.

I remember each night because of the mosquitoes and the occasional mango that let go from one of the trees above us. They always landed with a loud bang on our tin roof.

The first night, mosquitoes kept everyone awake as they feasted on our blood. For some reason, they didn't bother me as much as the rest of the family, who were getting eaten alive. The next day, they went to the local market to buy mosquito nets. I made fun of them for being so weak and didn't get one. That night, our little dog Quita and I were the only ones unprotected. I spent a miserable night as the sole source of blood for the swarms of biting insects. I braved it out, however, unwilling to admit I was wrong. Quita had no such pride and crawled under someone's net for protection. The next day, I bought a mosquito net, too.

Tres Valles was noteworthy for its precipitation. Each morning, we would wake up to a clear, blue sky. As the morning progressed, however, the clouds would begin to form. By noon, it was cloudy; by one, it was pouring rain. It would rain every afternoon for several hours and then stop. This cycle repeated every day like clockwork.

We made no friends, held no church services, and stayed out of school.

One morning, Dad announced that God had told him in a dream to pack up once again and go back to Los Ramones. We took the two-day trek back and rented the same house we had left two months earlier. The next day, we walked into school like nothing had happened.

Professor Melchor didn't say a word. He just looked at us and shook his head as we walked by. Since I had read all my textbooks out of sheer boredom, I caught up on my coursework immediately.

26

Sleeping in a Car

It's hard to get a good night's sleep sitting upright in a car. Especially if you're sitting in a hot car, shoulder to shoulder with three other people in the front seat...with oncoming headlights shining in your eyes every minute or so...and you're getting eaten alive by mosquitoes.

We learned about mosquito nets during our trip to Guatemala, and we sometimes draped them over the car to keep the mosquitoes out, but that only made it hotter inside.

In the early days, we had no such luxury. After the Old Truck conked out, Dad got the green 1956 Buick Special. It was a big car but not really big enough to allow our family to sleep inside; and before Althea and Dan left, that included five of us kids, Mom and Dad, and our dog. I was a little kid back in those days, but I still remember one particular night we were sitting in a roadside park just outside of Louise, Texas. It was summer, and we were very tired and trying to sleep.

I kept thinking, *I know Dad said he's exhausted, but I am so tired. If he'd only start the car and drive a few hours, the air would cool us off, and we could all get some sleep. Well, except for him, but that's* his *problem.*

Eventually, Dad got tired of sitting there, sweating and swatting mosquitoes and staring at the headlights of passing cars. He started up the car and drove.

I was asleep within minutes.

27

Lazarus

One winter, we were adopted by a small male cat. I named him Blackie.

One morning, Dad started up the car, and we heard this otherworldly caterwauling under the hood. The car stalled, and Dad opened the hood. Blackie flew out from under it, eyes wild and blood dripping. Apparently, he had crawled up onto the engine to sleep or get warm.

When we caught up with him, he was a bloody mess. Much of his fur and huge patches of skin were gone. He was barely alive. As usual, Mom took over the task of saving yet another creature's life. We nursed him back to health, but he never quite recovered.

When I would lie down to sleep at night, he would crawl under the covers all the way down to my feet. The cold bothered him the most and made him ache. Many a night, I would shift in my sleep; and suddenly, a black nightmare would explode under the blanket, screeching, clawing, and biting at my legs. But no matter how much it hurt, I always let him sleep with me.

He had been through enough.

For a short time, we had a travel trailer. It had a small kitchen, a bathroom, and bunk beds. It was quite a luxury for us. At one point while we were living in the adobe house in front of Porfirio's store, the trailer was parked in the backyard, and we lived in both quarters.

It had rained heavily for a few days and water stood four to five inches deep across the yard, so Dad set cinder blocks as stepping stones between the house and the trailer. That way, we could walk between the two living quarters without getting our pants soaked.

One afternoon, I hopped barefoot across the cinder blocks to the trailer and grabbed a metal handle to hoist myself in. Suddenly, it felt like a giant was ripping my arm out of its socket. I was being electrocuted.

I heard myself yelling, "AHHH! AHHH!" as I tried to let go of the handle, but my hand would not respond, and I couldn't loosen my grip. As the violence continued unabated, I felt like I was going to explode, and I began to lose consciousness.

Finally, as suddenly as it had started, it stopped, and I collapsed into the water with a splash.

I sensed Dad and Mom rushing out of the trailer. Dad picked me up and carried me into the house where he laid me on the bench by the dining table. I was faintly aware of him and Mom; but I had no strength in my body, no will of my own. Meanwhile, Mom was explaining that she had the presence of mind to switch off a light that apparently had been shorting out, which ended the attack.

Dad and Mom began fervently praying over me. I still sensed them at the edge of my consciousness, but I felt like I was in a deep dark tunnel. When Dad closed the prayer with "Amen," I felt the breath of life whoosh back into my lungs; and suddenly, I was alert and good as new.

28

Passing out the Gospel

D ad liked the Gospel of John best of all. He thought John, who was known as the disciple that Jesus loved, was the closest to understanding the God of Love. So he would buy little Evangelio de San Juan booklets by the case; and every once in awhile, we would get in the car and drive to a nearby town where we would go door to door to witness and pass out the little booklets. If someone invited us in, Dad would preach to them awhile.

I *hated* it.

For one thing, when I was around him, I felt like a caged animal. It seemed like everything I said was wrong. There were no conversations allowed that didn't involve God or Jesus or doing the right thing.

I didn't *want* to do the right thing—I just wanted to go play. And I couldn't figure out what we were doing or why. It made no sense. Every kid I knew in the United States was normal. They lived in houses. They ate real food—not damaged canned goods from the back of a grocery store or food that had been cooked over and over till it was gritty so it wouldn't spoil. They went to normal schools and ate in the school cafeteria—not peanut butter and jelly sandwiches made with course homemade bread. They played baseball and basketball and football. They even had TVs in their houses and watched cartoons every Saturday.

I couldn't imagine that.

The kids in Mexico were normal, too. They didn't live as well as the kids back home; but most had a mom and dad, went to school, lived in some kind of house, had chores, and played whatever game was in season. And although most of the families I knew didn't have a car, they got around just fine on foot or by bicycle.

They were all normal.

Not us. We ate weird food, wore hand-me-down clothes that didn't fit, and drove a car with embarrassing signs painted on it and a huge loudspeaker mounted on the top. And we had church services every single night in our house without exception. We were supposed to be examples of how to live, but I *hated* the way we lived.

So we would walk down the street and knock on people's doors and intrude upon their lives. Mostly, they were Catholic and happy being Catholic, and I couldn't understand what difference it really made. Dad's Spanish was really good now; but he never lost the gringo accent, which I found appalling; and he seemed to be looking for an area where they disagreed with him; and that's what he would talk about.

I now spoke like a Mexican, but I didn't care a whit for the topic of religion. It made no difference to me. God was God; Jesus was Jesus. So what were they arguing about? And I would longingly watch the kids playing cards or marbles or futbol in the street and wish I could join them. Instead, I was passing out booklets and pretending to care about God. It just seemed so pointless.

One day, I was particularly hot and thirsty. When we finished passing out booklets to each little shack in the village, we stopped at a little store with a few tables out front. Dad bought a can of sardines, a box of crackers, and a couple of Cokes, and we sat down at a card table outside the cafe and ate together.

Just me and my dad.

Turns out—it wasn't such a bad day after all.

⁓⁓⁓

Every town in Mexico has at least one beggar family, and Los Ramones was no exception. The family in our village had a mom and about seven kids who didn't go to school at all. I don't know if the dad died, ran off, or had simply crossed into the United States and never came back, but this family had no income and were very poor—even by Mexican village standards.

Dad always talked about caring for widows and the fatherless, so he decided our family was going to take on the beggar family. He invited them over every day; and they would come over, eat our food, wear our clothes, and stay. It got to where they were staying over *all* day, *every* day. Their mom would stay home, so there was no one to discipline or keep track of them. They just ran riot. In *our* house.

I highly resented them. I reasoned there wasn't enough food or clothing to begin with, and they ate like they had never eaten before. On top of that, we were required to play with them, and I didn't like that one bit. My best friend Carlos lived right over the backyard wall; and when they were at our house, he usually wouldn't come over.

One day, Dad decided he wasn't going to let them come over any more. The experiment was over. He gave no explanation, and I didn't care. I was just happy to get my life back.

Years later, Dad confided to me the reason he had stopped inviting the beggar family over was that God had showed him in a dream that he took better care of other people's kids than he did his own.

29

Blessed Rain

One summer, it was exceptionally hot and dry. None of the streets in Los Ramones were paved; so when it got that arid, everything was covered with dust. Since no one had air conditioning and all the homes were open, every time a car or a horse-drawn buggy worked its way down the street, the dust would billow into the houses and choke everyone who was there.

The hot wind blew down the streets, kicking up dust devils that would swirl around like mini-tornadoes, rearranging the dead weeds, trash, and dirt. The heat was relentless. When we walked barefoot on the street, our feet would sink ankle deep into scalding powder.

It didn't rain for nine months straight. There was no relief anywhere. Even the river dried up to a trickle with only a few pools—most too shallow to swim in.

We were now living in a two-room hut made of cinder blocks with a tin roof. We lived in one room, while the other was reserved for our nightly church services. Every time a cloud went by, the tin would tick as the metal contracted, then tick again as the sun returned.

There was a place a couple miles from town we called El Sabino where a huge cypress rose majestically from the river's edge. This tree was so big that three of us couldn't reach our arms around the trunk. It had knots on it, some which we used for handholds to climb, and others that were large enough to use as jumping off points. The pool underneath this beautiful tree was deep enough to dive into and shaded enough to be fairly cool, and we spent many of our lazy summer afternoons there.

The local livestock were not so fortunate. Without rain, not a blade of grass grew. When the tanks dried up, they had no water to drink. Circling buzzards marked the spots of the dying cattle and horses. Bleached bones dotted the fields and meadows. The local ranchers were forced to feed their cattle prickly pear cactus.

Prickly pear is a crucial part of life in Northern Mexico. *Nopal* is used in the dry areas for cattle feed. But the cows cannot eat it as it grows. The ranchers use kerosene torches to singe the spines off the cactus pads and then chop them up with machetes so they can feed their livestock. A dual benefit of feeding prickly pear to cattle is that it is 90 percent water, so livestock can go without fresh water for long periods of time. In this way, ranchers are able to save some of their cattle during prolonged droughts.

Prickly pear is also an important part of the Mexican diet. In the springtime, the cacti put out tender, bright green shoots, which are harvested, despined, and cut into strips and then sautéed with onions, tomatoes, and Serrano chile peppers, producing a delicious, nutritious dish called *nopalitos*. Nopal is often the sole green vegetable available to poor Mexican *campesino* and along with beans and tortillas completes a staple diet.

During this particular summer, the drought was so unrelenting that not only did the stock tanks and vegetation dry up, even the prickly pear, typically so abundant to the area, was soon depleted.

⸺⧔⸺

Los Ramones is on a slight rise; and one particularly hot morning way off to the north and barely above the horizon, we began to see dark clouds forming. They were probably a hundred miles away and hardly moving, and we watched them inch closer ever so slowly throughout the day.

Along toward early afternoon, we began to smell petrichor—that heavenly fragrance produced when much-needed rain falls on parched ground. Since there had been several close calls with storm clouds passing us by, everyone was antsy. It seemed everyone, man and beast, had been craving the cooling rains. Could this be the long-awaited day when we would finally get relief from the chokehold the drought had put on us?

Midafternoon, the sky got very dark—almost green. All of a sudden, the storm clouds were upon us. A breeze began to pick up; it wasn't that hot wind that dried everything in its path—it was cool, almost cold.

I stood in the street, waiting eagerly for the first drops of rain, wondering: *Will the rain ever come?* I was afraid to even hope for it—I feared it would just blow on by without raining a single drop like some cruel trick played on us.

Plop! Suddenly, a huge drop hit the ground, kicking up a little cloud of dust. Then another. And another. Soon huge drops were pelting the street as the breeze picked up speed to a now-gusty wind, blowing huge clouds of dust up the main thoroughfare. Children wild with excitement screeched loudly; older people eagerly looked to the sky. With faces full of hope, everyone stepped up their pace to reach shelter before the storm hit.

A bolt of lightning suddenly crashed down from the sky. The roar of the ensuing downpour on steaming tin roofs mixed with shrieks and laughter as people ran for cover and children stomped through the now-forming puddles. No one really cared if they got wet. The whole town was one giant celebration.

Swiftly, a stream formed and began running down the street, first as a trickle and then a river. The water got so deep, we laid in it and let it carry us away. We splashed, ran, and rolled in the filthy brine, overjoyed to be cool at last.

After an hour or so, the rain slowed to a steady downpour that continued through the night. The pitter-patter of raindrops on the tin roof along with the refreshing cool air made it comfortable enough to require a sheet for cover. I slept better than I had in months.

⸺✦⸺

A few days later, we had a solar eclipse. Dad taught us kids how to poke a hole in a sheet of cardboard and look at the shape of the hole on the ground. Whereas the hole normally would create a round bit of light at our feet, as the moon blotted out more and more of the sun during the eclipse, the light shining through the hole began to look like a quarter moon. He warned us not to look at the sun through smoked glass, as some people were doing, or we could damage our eyes and ruin our vision.

Later on, Carlos came over. We were bored with nothing to do, so we walked down the street to buy Cokes at Don Porfirio's corner store. His store had a window that was covered with steel bars through which we could see merchandise. There was nothing we really wanted; but items were there for the taking; and we discovered that if we stuck two fingers through the bars, we could reach some packets of navy blue clothing dye.

We worked several of the dye packets out between the bars, wondering what we were going to do with them. Just like we sometimes vandalized for fun, we often stole things for pure entertainment.

After finishing our Cokes, we took off, wandering down the street, trying to think of something fun to do with our new-found treasure. There were still pools of standing water in the street from the recent rain; and we came upon a huge puddle, probably twelve or fourteen feet across, and decided to dump one of the dye packets in to see what would happen.

The entire puddle turned a deep blue.

Two women and a bunch of kids walked towards us as we stood there admiring our handiwork. When the family came by, Carlos said in a voice loud enough that they could hear, "Look what the eclipse did to that mud puddle!"

The women and children stopped and stared, and then they began talking excitedly to each other. As others came by, they talked to them, too. Pretty soon there was a small group of people standing by the mud puddle, talking, gesturing excitedly, and pointing at the puddle of blue water.

We decided to ramp it up.

Rio Pesqueria was a block away. It wasn't really much of a river—more like a creek—and it had been so dry that there was barely a trickle between pools of water. Carlos and I went down to the river and dumped the rest of the dye into it.

The entire stream between pools turned blue.

We went back up the river bank and stood there, looking at the river, waiting for people to walk by. As a group approached, we exclaimed excitedly, "Look what the eclipse did! It turned the river blue!"

By now a large group was starting to gather, pointing and talking excitedly. We were whipping up the crowd when our friend Denny happened by.

We tried to pull the same stunt on him, but he wasn't buying it. He smelled a rat. He walked down to the water's edge and spotted the empty dye envelopes.

Our game was up.

30

Hard Labor

Every six months, we were required to leave Mexico and stay out of the country for a minimum of two weeks before we could go back. This meant leaving school, coming to the States, and waiting for a few weeks to go by.

If we were planning on going back into Mexico, we would typically camp at Bentsen-Rio Grande Valley State Park. I liked it there because we had running water and showers, and there was a nice-sized lake to fish. It was also home to the green jay, a beautiful bird said to be found nowhere else in the United States.

One of the people we met while we were living in the state park was a man named Jesus Larios. He was a maintenance man, and he had a family. I quickly became friends with his oldest son Lupe, who was my age. That was pure heaven. Not only did they have a TV, but his mom, Esperanza, cooked incredible food. There were two other children younger than Lupe: Faustina, who I had a crush on, and Chucho. These people treated me like family, and sometimes Dad would let me go over to their house on Saturday mornings and watch cartoons. When we were in the States, I hung out with them whenever I could.

When I was fourteen, I got it into my head that I wanted to work. Money meant freedom to me, and I was eager to earn some. At that point, we were staying at a trailer park, camped out in a tent. The owner of the park asked me if I wanted to earn some money digging septic ditches by hand. I said sure.

I weighed every bit of 120 pounds at that point, and digging those holes was much harder than I thought it would be. I had to use a pick to loosen the clay and then shovel the dirt out. I soon developed blisters on my hands, and I wasn't even six inches down.

After a while, Dad came over and started helping me. Being the self-centered person that I am, I decided he took over the project so he could take my money.

I became sullen and resentful. I'll never forget the hurt look on his face as I pouted and sulked.

We finished the project and got paid, and he gave me the money.

I quickly spent it on a Daisy pellet rifle.

———

Since Lupe and his family were migrant workers, I asked them if I could go with them to the fields to earn money. We were hired to thin out pepper plants. All of us worked in the fields, down to Chucho, who was only ten years old.

It was the hardest work I have ever done.

We were given hoes with two-foot handles and instructed to leave one or two plants every eight inches. The handles were short so that workers wouldn't stop and lean on them. It was explained to me that this increased laborers' productivity.

We worked for a dollar an hour, ten hours a day, for five days in the South Texas heat. I was so tired at the end of each day that I had to sleep with my arms extended over my head to keep my shoulders from cramping. I had nightmares every night; but each morning, I went back to work.

At the end of five days, we were paid.

Since I was the only white person in my group, I was given the wages for everyone, and it was up to me to decide if I wanted to keep all the money or pay the Larios family. Of course I paid them, but it was an eye opener for me to see how often these beautiful people were exploited.

I made fifty bucks that week—a huge amount of money.

We left for Mexico soon after that. When we got back to the little house we were renting in Los Ramones, I hid that money in the pocket of my winter jacket where no one would find it.

31

Jailbird

We had just come back from the States where I had earned some money, and I was enjoying life. Carlos had moved to Monterrey; but he was back for a visit; and he, our friend Gerardo, and I decided to go hunting.

Gerardo had his mom's .22 rifle, Carlos had a slingshot, and I had my brand new Daisy pellet rifle. We hunted all day, hoping for a rabbit or two, but we saw no game, so we started shooting at different things. One of our targets was a tractor whose headlights we found irresistible. We shot them out.

The next day while we were hanging out at my house, the police came by. Carlos was in the outhouse in the backyard; and when he saw the cop car, he took off in the other direction. The deputy searched the house and confiscated my pellet rifle. Then off to jail Gerardo and I went.

I wasn't sure why we were being arrested. Vandalism was an everyday thing for us. It was what we did for fun, so it was anybody's guess why we had been nabbed. The deputy wouldn't tell us, and we didn't volunteer anything. What followed was a long day in the county jail. I didn't like it. Even though Gerardo and I were alone in the cell, it was still pretty scary.

Along toward the end of the day, Dad strode into the jail. "They say you shot out some tractor headlights," he said. "I just want to know one thing: Did you do it?"

"Yes," I answered.

Without another word, he turned on his heel and walked out.

About an hour later, he came back, and they let us out of jail. He didn't say a word. All the way home, I wondered who had paid the fine. As quickly as possible, I went to check my secret hiding place where I kept the money from my summer job.

It was gone.

That was one of the best and toughest lessons I ever learned.

32

The Serpent

Since I had paid the fine with my own money, Dad gave the pellet rifle back to me. I had learned my lesson, and I think he trusted that I wouldn't do anything to jeopardize his trust.

I loved that gun. It had a shiny blue metal barrel and a genuine wood stock, which I polished to a high sheen with an oily rag. It could shoot either regular BBs or .177 pellets. Since the pellets were slightly heavier, I preferred them. Dad helped me adjust the sights. It was a very accurate little gun, and I began using it in earnest. It was excellent for dove hunting, and doves meant food.

At first, I would simply aim at the center mass of the dove itself; but after hitting them and having them fly far enough away that I couldn't find them, I decided to settle for head shots. I hated the thought of an injured bird in pain and dying; and by aiming for the head, I would either hit them and they'd drop straight down, or if I missed them, they could fly away unharmed. I was an excellent shot and bagged many a bit of protein in that manner.

I also used my gun for duck hunting, which in Mexico is nothing like it is here. No one I knew had a shotgun, so it was necessary to sneak up on the ducks while they were sitting on a waterhole and pick them off the water.

One cold winter day, I tiptoed up to a pond, hid behind some bushes, and slowly peered through them. Out in the middle of the pool was a lone male mallard looking so handsome with his blue-green head. He was so far away that I had to aim about a foot above him to compensate for the drop. I found a branch to steady the rifle on, took aim, and pulled the trigger. Much to my surprise, I hit him dead on.

I soon realized I was going to have to retrieve him, and that meant swimming out in the frigid water. I wasn't about to let my prize go; so I stripped down, swam out, grabbed him, and swam back. I was freezing cold as I put my clothes back on and happy to head home.

When I showed my prize to Dad and asked him how to cook it, he said, "Well, first, you get a cutting board and dress the duck on that cutting board. You cut its head off, pull the feathers off, take out the insides, and wash it down. Then you feed the duck to the dog and cook up the cutting board. This is the best way to enjoy eating wild duck."

Months later, I was hunting down by the arroyo a few miles from home. Through the dense foliage surrounding the small river, I could see some ducks sitting on a pool of water. As I inched my way closer to get a clear shot, I heard *it*.

If you've never heard *it*, let me tell you, there is nothing quite like it.

If you *have* heard *it*, it will stay with you forever. I promise; you will never forget.

First of all, it's *urgent*. You can't ignore it. You can't just say, "I'm not going to break my concentration. I'm going to get that duck!" It's not like you can pause, look around until you spot it, and say, "Why hello, Mister Diamondback! Don't mind me! I'll be gone in a few minutes!" No. Immediate action is required.

I heard the rattle clearly.

I had no idea what direction it was coming from or how far away it was, but I was 100 percent clear exactly what predator I was dealing with. It sounded like it was right underfoot; but it could have been anywhere, in any direction.

After a second, it stopped.

I froze and felt the blood rush to my head as goose bumps ran up and down my spine. My hair literally felt like it was standing straight up, and I wanted to run as fast as I could, but I didn't know which direction to run! I was petrified.

Another half second passed. I screamed in terror, jumped as far as I could, and took off running. The ducks loudly took flight behind me while I hoped against hope that I was running away—not toward—it, expecting at any moment to feel that whiplash on my leg followed by excruciating pain. I could see myself falling to the ground and writhing in agony while the evil rattler took it's time, slowly slithering over my petrified body to look me in the eye before finishing me off.

But I had guessed right and jumped in the right direction.

I lived to see another day.

33

God's Messenger

One day, Dad called us all together for a family meeting. By this time, Dan had moved to New York for a farm deferment to avoid being drafted to serve in Vietnam, and Althea had eloped and was married. So along with Dad and Mom, only Ruth, Martha, and I remained.

Dad announced that he was going to get Mom pregnant and have a "pure" baby—and instead of letting Mom go to a doctor, he was going to deliver the baby himself. He reasoned that he had delivered hundreds of calves as a dairy farmer and couldn't see how this could be much different.

Dad believed that going to a doctor constituted a lack of faith. That is why we were never allowed to seek medical care, no matter how sick we were, and why we weren't allowed to take aspirin for a headache.

That is also why Dad never took Martha to a doctor to see why she couldn't hear or speak and why he never allowed anyone to teach her sign language. He insisted that God was going to heal her some day.

As I've said before, Dad was big on faith.

But there was a major flaw in Dad's religious conviction—each of us kids, including Martha, had been born in hospitals. And for that reason, Dad felt we were not a good testimony to "the truth." In fact, he blamed Mom for Martha's disabilities. I believe that is where the "pure child" theory was born. Because Martha wasn't getting healed, Dad reasoned that God would not heal her because Mom had insisted, and he had relented, to having Martha born in a hospital.

So Dad called us together to announce that we were "impure."

Impure because we had been tainted by a lack of faith.

Impure because we had been contaminated by worldly medicine.

This new child would be the ultimate proof that God was on our side, that the use of modern medicine constituted a lack of faith, and that Dad was a powerful and accurate messenger of God's true intent.

By now, Mom was thirty-nine years old, but she got pregnant. During her pregnancy, she kept eating chunks off the adobe walls of the shack we lived in. Dad would berate her for it, but she wouldn't stop. My guess is she had some kind of mineral deficiency, but that didn't seem to matter to him. He saw it as a sign of weakness. Once I came around the corner of the house to see her with mud on her mouth.

Busted. Ashamed.

After nine months, Sammy was born. As promised, Dad delivered him.

Sammy was a beautiful, smart, charming baby. It was a whole new experience having him toddle around. Mom was happy, it seemed, for the first time ever. Her days of screaming, "One of these days, I'm gonna walk out that door and never come back!" appeared to be over.

34

My Brother's Keeper

Dad decided we needed to go to Chihuahua, Mexico. I am not sure why. It seemed to be another one of those pointless trips I had come to know so well. I would come home from school or fishing, and Dad would say, "Get your stuff—we're leaving," followed by an endless explanation of why we were leaving that always started with, "The Lord told me in a dream last night..." And within hours, we'd be on the road again—another road to nowhere.

So we headed for Chihuahua, and it was hot. Most of Mexico is hot; but Chihuahua is high desert; and it was so hot, the sky had a silver color to it. It seemed there was no specific spot in the sky where the sun was—it seemed the whole sky was the sun. Riding in the car with the windows down and the air loud and hot, everything dried out. The air was thinner than I was used to, and it hurt to breathe. I suffered from frequent nose bleeds.

We took a little detour through a place called La Boquilla del Conchos, an area with a lake near Camargo, Mexico. This was promising. It was a beautiful place with water everywhere, and it looked so cool and refreshing. There was a little settlement just below the earthen dam; and because of poor engineering, I suppose, there were springs everywhere, with creeks and rivers leaking through, flowing downstream toward the bigger river below. There were trees everywhere, and taco stands, and little huts. The people were poor, but they seemed happy. This place looked like a resort for peasants.

As we explored the area, the car ground to a stop. We had a broken U-joint. Of course, all our earthly possessions were in the car, so we had to find a place where we could unload. It was almost impossible to jack up that huge car loaded to the gills with our stuff.

Next to the road where we had come to a stop was a shack made of sticks and mud with a thatched roof and a concrete floor. And it was vacant. Perfect! We found the owner and offered him a few American dollars to let us stay there as long as we needed while we fixed the car.

Dad set off to find a ride to town to begin his search for the part. Meanwhile, I went exploring. I was sixteen years old now, rebellious and angry and given to doing my own thing. I didn't like staying with the family; and whenever possible, I avoided working with Dad because of his temper. So I managed to get away.

This place felt like heaven. First of all, there was water everywhere, and water meant fish, and fish meant food, and no one fried a better filet than Mom. Whenever I could catch a fish, Mom would set up the camp stove, get out the frying pan, and dinner was on the way.

During my scouting trip, I met some kids my age—a boy and his girlfriend and a girl who came along to keep an eye on them. She and I hit it off instantly; and I spent the entire afternoon exploring the landscape with Marina and her friends, Pablo and Gizela. Dad had never allowed me to date; so I had never even held hands, let alone kissed a girl. And here I was in paradise, holding hands with Marina, jumping puddles, and exploring swimming holes that we dove into, fully clothed. I couldn't remember ever being so happy. I was in love!

That evening when I came back, Dad was still working on the car, and Mom was holding Sammy. By now, Sammy was about thirty months old. He was complaining about his side hurting. We had seen Mom pick him up by his little arm, so we assumed he had a strained muscle or something. I really didn't pay much attention—it was pretty common for us to have aches and pains. Besides, I was in love. Nothing was going to ruin my day.

Three days later when I came home after spending the day with my new friends, Mom was still holding Sammy. He was very ill, and the talk was that Dad had killed two black widow spiders in the shack we were now calling home. The man who rented us the hut had come by, taken one look at Sammy, and told Dad that if we didn't get him to the doctor, he was going to die.

I wasn't too worried. Sammy was pure. Dad had told us over and over that nothing could happen to him because he had been born in faith. Mom looked worried, but Mom was a worrier.

On the fifth day, I was with my new friends when Ruth came to find me. Mom had sent for me. Ruth said Sammy was dying. This was the first time I ever really considered how sick he was, and I rushed to the shack. Mom was rocking him, my sisters and Dad were standing around, and Dad was praying. Suddenly, the urgency of the situation struck me, and I was terrified. Sammy could die!

Soon we were all praying loudly, frantically, because Sammy seemed to be losing his fight for life.

On July 21, 1971, at about one o'clock in the afternoon, Sammy died.

At first, we couldn't believe it. *How could a child be so full of life one minute and dead the next? Where did he go?*

Dad told Mom to lay Sammy down on the floor. "This is the big test!" he yelled. "Keep the faith up!" Then he began shouting, "Satan, in the name of Jesus, I rebuke you! Sammy, in the name of Jesus, I command you to stand up and walk!"

By now, we were all crying; and Dad reprimanded us, "Don't *cry!* That is a lack of faith! Have *faith!*"

Then he turned to Sammy and roared, "Samuel David Moore, STAND UP AND WALK IN THE NAME OF JESUS! It is written, 'and he healed them every one!'" Then Dad got out the olive oil and anointed Sammy's head, shouting, "SATAN, *GET OUT OF SAMMY AND LEAVE HIM ALONE!* For it is written, 'And I will give unto thee the keys of the kingdom of heaven: and whatsoever thou shalt bind on earth shall be bound in heaven: and whatsoever thou shalt loose on earth shall be loosed in heaven!'"

Nothing.

After about an hour or so of this, Dad finally gave up. He allowed us to cry.

"I don't understand how this could happen!" he said. "We did it *right!*"

But Sammy was still lying on the cement floor. Dead.

Mom picked him up and cradled him. She kissed him and held him. Then she took off his shirt. There were two spider bites—one on the inside of his arm, and the other on his little chest. That was the first time I had seen them.

As I stood there, numb, watching Mom and Sammy, I notice our new dog staring at my baby brother. Suddenly, the dog jumped up and started barking furiously at something only he could see—something that came out of Sammy. Whatever it was, the dog followed it with his eyes as it rose and then chased it out the open door. I don't know if anyone else saw what I saw, but I know that dog was barking at something. Maybe it was Sammy's soul.

By now, Dad was once again in motion. The car had been fixed earlier that afternoon, and Dad carried

Sammy's body to the car. Then he and Mom and the girls took off for the funeral home in the nearest town.

I was alone.

All happiness I felt about my innocent love with Marina was gone—replaced with enormous guilt. *How could I have let this happen? What kind of a big brother was I? If I had been a good big brother, I would somehow have saved Sammy's life. Sammy was dying while I was off messing around with a girl!*

There was a beautiful place nearby. It was a ledge over a pond. I had happily stood there several times in the past five days, admiring the view, thinking of my new girl, enjoying my new-found happiness. I saw no beauty there now. All I saw was my guilt. My shame.

I began to pray.

Dear God, how could You let this happen? Everyone knows I am the evil son, and Sammy is the good one.

I am the impure one, and Sammy is pure.

Please bring Sammy back and take me.

I will suffer whatever I have to suffer, but please *bring him back.*

My answer was silence.

I could see my whole life shattered. Our reason to be was a farce. My entire life had been the life of a missionary, living on faith, proving that God took care of His own, favoring us above all others because of our faith; and yet, He had taken Sammy, the pure one, and left me, Benjamin, the evil one.

I felt anguish like never before.

Several hours later, Dad and Mom and the girls returned with Sammy. He had been embalmed and put in a little white casket. It was about three feet long, and it was on the wooden ledge Dad had built between the back of the front seat and the back window.

There are no words to describe the devastation we felt. Hardly anyone could say a word; but in bits and pieces, I gathered that Dad wanted to bury Sammy back in Los Ramones, the town of his birth. I guess it was the closest thing to home we had ever known. However, Los Ramones was a two-day and two-night drive from where we were.

We loaded up the car with Sammy on the back ledge and took off. I never even got to tell Marina goodbye. The car smelled of dust, grief, and embalming fluid. It was suffocating.

No one spoke.

As I stared out at the now-darkened landscape and watched the lights go by, I tried to understand...and I wished I wasn't a murderer.

35

Damned

We arrived in Los Ramones two days later. Dad
rented the little house we had left several weeks
earlier, and then he held a funeral service for
Sammy in the little chapel that occupied the front room.
I don't remember a word Dad said. I was choked with
agony and defeat.

Afterward, four pallbearers, including me, slowly
carried Sammy's tiny casket down the dusty, unpaved
street past little stucco and adobe huts with the *novela*
(soap opera) blaring through open doors and windows.
Down the main street, out of town, to the local cemetery
we went with a procession of sweaty, barefoot children
and men in dirty clothes and huaraches. It was very hot,

right in the middle of summer; and the smells of embalming fluid, mesquite fires, beans, onions, and cow manure filled the air. After a short graveside service, led of course by Dad, we buried Sammy in a little plot. I threw the first handful of soil into the hole and along with it, my joy, my faith, and my soul.

Up until Sammy's death, I had many doubts about Dad's behavior and his ability to adhere to his own teachings, but I had never thrown them out completely. I believed that much of what he taught was true, and I admired him for being willing to go to any length to stay faithful to what he saw as God's real message. But at that moment in my life, I rejected almost everything he taught. I was openly defiant of him.

I was bitter and angry with him for not taking Sammy to a doctor when he had been bitten by a spider. I believed Sammy's death was proof that doctors were put here on earth to do good, and Dad's insistence that using medicine signified a lack of faith simply could not be true.

I was angry with God for not intervening on Sammy's behalf because had He done so, my baby brother would still be alive.

And of course, I was consumed with guilt for not having saved him myself.

Months passed. It was the Christmas season. Up until that year, Christmas had been a joyous time for our family. It was the time of year when the weather was cool; it was the time of year when we got a big box from Grandma filled with much-needed hand-me-downs collected from my cousins back home.

Christmas time had always been my favorite time of year. I especially loved the music. We sang carols during our services instead of the usual hymns and played classical Christmas music on the loudspeakers. The Christmas before whenever Handel's *Messiah* was playing, little Sammy would sing, "Ah yu yah...Ah yu yah..." until the record advanced to the next song. Then he would yell, "AH YU YAH!" one more time, and you'd hear *rrrrrrripppp!* as he dragged the needle across the vinyl record to play the song again.

This Christmas, there was none of that joy.

Mom was deeply depressed and walked with the gait of a much older person. Her eyes were vacant and hollow.

Dad talked and talked, trying to reason out what had happened, attempting to convince Mom we did the right thing. Mom would nod listlessly; and when Dad insisted on a response, she would reply, "Yes, Dear...."

There were many tearful nights when Dad talked about Sammy being in heaven. On one occasion while rummaging through his tool box, he came across a toy wrench Sammy had left there; and he began to cry, tears dripping down his nose.

I didn't cry.

All my grief was funneled into hating Dad.

In my eyes, Dad had killed Sammy and had wrenched from Mom any happiness she had ever known in our bleak existence. In effect, he had killed us all. I dreamed of taking Mom away from him.

For his part, Dad never outwardly questioned himself or his beliefs. He just plodded on.

Before Sammy died, I had been ordained a minister in our church. I suppose it had not been that formal, really, as Dad declared me a minister, but I had given Jesus the marriage vows and dedicated my life to Him, and that meant being a teacher of the Word. Now Dad was asking me to preach. Despite the fact my heart was no longer in it, Dad insisted I become more of a leader in our little gatherings.

One day in April 1972, he received a letter from the Texas Department of Motor Vehicles, and he decided he needed to go back and take care of some paperwork involving our car. The plan was for Dad, Mom, Ruth, and Martha to go to Texas for a week or so, and I would stay behind and hold nightly services while they were gone.

We laid out some homemade church pews in my friend Eugenio's yard and hung a string of lights. Then Dad gave me $120 of God's money and instructed me to preach. This was a lot of money. Our family had lived on $175 a month and sometimes far less for years.

I was still grieving Sammy's death. I no longer supported Dad's ministry, and I was no longer inspired by the vision I'd had as an eleven year old to bring thousands of people to the truth that God is love. I felt completely alienated from God. I was angry with Him for taking Sammy and still couldn't understand why He hadn't taken me instead. Everyone knew I was the bad son, and I knew God didn't love me and certainly didn't watch over me. I had nothing to contribute to others on the topic of God. In fact, I saw no difference between God and Dad, and I didn't want to have anything to do with either one of them.

I couldn't bring myself to hold a church service. Every day, I would tell myself, "Tonight, I will have a service." And every night, eight o'clock would come and go, and I wouldn't lift a finger. Then I'd tell myself, "Tomorrow, I will have a service."

I never did.

⤳✵⤺

During the time they were gone, I had my seventeenth birthday. For the first time in my life, I was free to come and go as I pleased, and I had more money in my pocket than I had ever seen before, so I decided to celebrate. I bought two bottles of tequila with God's money and had a party.

I don't recall much about that night. I do remember I was the center of attention. Everyone laughed at my jokes, and there was a girl several years older than I who followed me around and egged me on. She seemed to flirt with me, and somehow I was hers that night. There were other girls, too. I don't even know where they came from or how they found out about my little party, but there they were.

I started drinking tequila like it was Kool-Aid and soon became gloriously drunk. I vaguely remember being on all fours in someone's backyard, puking my guts out. My little friend suddenly disappeared; and when I came to the next morning, I was laying on the local dentist's couch. Since I had never met this man, at least that I remember, I quietly let myself out without saying goodbye.

I had always thought that reality was fixed; but that night, I discovered reality is a perception; and my normal reality, which was one of intense misery, was one I could change at will if I drank. It was awesome. I decided to drink every chance I got and to drink until I was drunk.

As the time for Dad's return neared, though, I became morose, increasingly guilty, and just plain terrified. *How was I going to explain all this to him?* Of all the people in the world, he was the one who frightened me the most. And in a small town, it would only be a matter of hours before he found out about my drunken escapade.

And of course, he did.

I don't recall any real consequences, though. I guess Dad had given up on me by now; so aside from a good chewing out, nothing else happened.

More troubling to me was that I had used God's money, entrusted to me to forward His Kingdom here on earth, to get drunk. In my mind, there was no excuse for this. There was no forgiveness possible.

I was damned to hell forever.

36

Hell

After Sammy's death, Eugenio became my new best friend. Carlos and Gerardo had moved to Monterrey a few years earlier, and Eugenio was attending our church services on a regular basis. I'm pretty sure he had his eye on my little sister Ruth.

When Mom and Dad went to Texas to take care of the car, I moved in for a few weeks with Eugenio and his family. Eugenio lived in a standard adobe shack with a thatched roof and dirt floor. There was a kitchen, which served as the dining room, and a bedroom on either side. Since there was no running water, the restroom was an outhouse located in the backyard. When someone wanted to take a bath, they drew a bucket of water from the well and went behind the door in the kitchen where they used a tin can to pour water on themselves. Eugenio's mom, Doña Lupe, had one luxury—an adobe oven outside in the yard, where she would bake *bizcochos*—little breakfast biscuits—which she then sold for much-needed cash.

Eugenio and his younger brother Artemio were close to my age. They were followed by five kids whose names I don't remember. Doña Lupe had recently lost her husband to a heart attack and was in an impossibly desperate situation trying to feed her family. She was more than happy to take me in since I could provide a few American dollars to help.

I slept on the floor with the rest of the kids and ate at their table. The food was delicious, even if the accommodations were modest. Doña Lupe didn't have a salt shaker; so if you needed salt, you reached for a pinch from a bowl and sprinkled it on your food. She didn't have silverware, so I learned to eat using a tortilla as a spoon.

Doña Lupe always had a bowl of pickled piquin chilies on the table. Piquin chilies are tiny powerhouses about the size of English peas. They grow wild in northern Mexico and really pack a punch. While living with Eugenio, I learned how to eat them—you tuck one in a mouthful of food and make sure that when you chew, you always have a bit of food around the crushed little fellow. We regularly had contests to see who could eat the most chilies. I really enjoyed my time with that family. I didn't feel that pent-up tension I was so accustomed to in my own home, and I always felt welcome.

The summer after I moved out, Doña Lupe finally lost the house and was forced to move her entire family to Monterrey so she could find some kind of work. She had very few options. She was a widow with a second-grade education and could barely read or write. Since she had no family in Monterrey, she moved her children to a shantytown, about twenty miles outside the city.

Many people in America have heard the word *shantytown*, but very few Americans have actually experienced one.

I did.

First of all, most of rural Mexico is poor. There is very little work. Most families, unless they have close relatives with work in the United States to support them, have very little to eat. Meat twice a week is considered living well. This might be a cut of goat meat from the market or a rabbit shot while hunting. Many families raise a few chickens, so eggs are common as well as the occasional young pullet for dinner. Beans, nopalitos, tortillas, and chili peppers, along with seasonal fruits, are the staple diet.

The homes they live in are usually adobe structures with thatched roofs and dirt floors. The more modern buildings are made of cinder blocks with a cement floor and tin roof. There is usually no running water. There are seldom kitchen appliances. Cooking is done over a raised fireplace. Typically, there is an outhouse in the backyard; and water is hauled by bucket, either from a well or public spigots below street level. This is considered normal, and people live contented lives under these conditions. Most Americans would find this way of life impossible.

Shantytown living is poverty at a devastating new level.

I went to visit Doña Lupe a few months after she had moved away from Los Ramones. The new "house" she and her family lived in consisted of a full-size mattress with a loose structure of corrugated tin exactly the size of that mattress propped up on three sides. There was a fourth piece of tin overhead that served to keep the rain out. The "front" of the structure was open. Facing the open part of this hovel was a hole in the ground—a fire pit—where Doña Lupe did the cooking.

By now, Eugenio and Artemio had left home and were looking for work in the city. Doña Lupe and the rest of her children lived in the shanty. It was one of thousands of similar buildings erected on hundreds of acres of cow pastures. There were no streets—just pathways between little hovels—and no street lights. The only light at night came from the fire pits. There was no electricity, no running water, no plumbing of any kind. With no bathrooms and no sanitation, people just squatted out in the open to urinate and defecate. All water hauled by bucket from the nearby river was completely polluted with raw sewage runoff from this and similar settlements upstream; and when it rained, the entire place turned into a slippery, toxic mud hole.

Mangy dogs, chickens, pigs, and an occasional goat roamed free. There were flies everywhere. The mattress in Doña Lupe's "home" was infested with fleas, cockroaches, and bedbugs, and the mosquitoes were fierce. It was difficult to stay long for my visit—the stench of raw sewage and rotting garbage was overpowering and inescapable. Everywhere you looked, in all directions, as far as the eye could see, were people who wore either the alert look of a predator or the vacant stare of a victim resigned to fate.

At night, Doña Lupe slept on the filthy, bare mattress with as many kids as she could fit with her. The rest slept on the ground in front of the bed. They all slept in the clothes on their backs.

Doña Lupe had found work at the Holiday Inn, one of the high-rise hotels in downtown Monterrey. Each morning before dawn, she would rise, leave her sleeping children unattended, and pick her way in the dark between shanties and people sleeping on the ground to the highway. There she would catch a bus for a two-hour ride to the city, work a twelve-hour day, and then take the bus ride back to care for her family. She did this every day—day after day after day. What difficult choices she had to make. How worried she must have been leaving her helpless children alone in that shit hole. But I saw no self-pity on her face. Doña Lupe showed more courage in one hour of living in those conditions than most people I know show in a lifetime.

A few months after my visit, I heard that Doña Lupe had been killed—run over by a bus—while trying in the dark to get to work. I do not know what happened to her kids. Three of them were under five years of age. One day, their mom just never came home.

Many in the United States are outraged that people come illegally into this country. "They don't respect our laws!" they will say. But what law is more fundamental than the law that compels a mother or father to feed their children? And who among us, if our children were starving, wouldn't steal a loaf of bread to feed them? Some laws supersede others, but the obligation of parents to feed their children trumps them all.

Some may say (on a full stomach), "Well, why do they have so many children in the first place, if they can't feed them?" That is a valid question. The answer is that in a country with no social security, your children are your social security; and if the infant mortality rate is high, you have enough kids so that some of them will survive long enough to take care of you when you can no longer work.

I have seen the desperate poverty that can take over a family or a community. It sucks the very humanity out of people caught in its clutches. Human beings become less than animals. There is no morality when your children are starving, their bellies distended with worms. There is no dignity when you have to urinate and defecate in public. Who will defend you when your neighbor wants to use you for sex? Who will defend your children when you are off working and your neighbor wants to use them for sex? When immigrants show up in our country, for the most part, their only desire is to work, feed their children, and provide for their most basic needs—needs that we in America take for granted. They simply want the opportunities of a better life and a safe place to live.

I am unable to blame them for even a minute for coming to this country. I know these people.

Send them home?

Home to *where?*

37

Almost Home

Later that summer, Dad decided we should head to New York to visit Grandma again. It had been several years since we had been back home.

I had now been away for the better part of fourteen years. I was dark brown from being in the tropical sun, struggling somewhat with my English, and shell-shocked from the ordeal we had been through losing Sammy.

I did not belong to Mexico where I had grown up but never quite fit in because I was still a gringo. On the other hand, I didn't understand the home I had left so long ago. I was a stranger caught between a somewhat bizarre upbringing in a foreign culture and the home of my birth that was now more foreign than the one I had left. I was a "third culture kid"—a term coined by sociologists John and Ruth Useem to describe children who grow up in a foreign place and cannot relate to their home or host cultures. This is an experience common to children of military personnel, and it is an experience common to the children of missionaries.

After visiting with Grandma for a while and saying hello to my cousins, I walked over to the farm next door to see Tom. It had been three years; but as always, he was glad to see me. I was now a tad bit taller than he; and although I still couldn't grow sideburns, I didn't feel like such a pip-squeak standing next to him. We quickly caught up on our lives since we had last seen each other.

By now, smoking and drinking were a regular part of Tom's teenage life, and they quickly became part of mine. I spent most of my time with Tom and our friends Mike and Donny. We roamed the countryside; tinkered with cars; and worked on the farm, milking, haying, and performing other chores. It was good to be home.

After about two weeks, Dad started packing up the car. Our visit to Grandma's was coming to a close. When he saw me, he said, "Get your stuff together. It's time to head back."

Knowing this was coming, I had fortified myself with two shots of Jack Daniels. "I'm staying here," I said. And I came up with every excuse I could think of: I fearfully explained that I wanted to finish high school; I told him I eventually wanted to get married. I knew in my heart there was nothing he could say to change my mind—I was never getting back in that car again.

I asked Grandma if I could stay with her. After consulting with Dad, she said yes. She said I could stay in Dan's old bedroom where he had roomed when he came up on his farm deferment. We decided that, come September, I would enroll in high school and graduate.

Dad didn't like it, but my mind was made up. I finished watching him pack. The next day when he, Mom, Ruth, and Martha got in the car and drove away, I let out a sigh of relief.

<hr/>

Decisions made by a child, regardless of how senseless they are, shape the life of the decision maker; and like a judge passing down a sentence on an offender, each time I made a poor decision, I sentenced myself.

By the time I was seventeen, I had sentenced myself to the life of a bad boy, a coward, a vandal, a thief, a traitor, a murderer, and a drunk; I was impure and damned.

I was racked by guilt for having been too demanding about my basic needs, like having enough to eat; for having stolen exams in school; for the endless lies and thefts and destroyed property I had perpetrated against others; for failing to protect Boy; for failing to save Sammy; and for using God's money to get drunk. I had pretended I was tough but refused to fight, knowing inside I was really a coward. I acted like I was smart but was afraid I might be stupid. And I was so desperate for the attention of a female that I was willing to give myself to anyone who would have me. Finally, I presented myself as a Christian, knowing inside I was a "backslider," wanting nothing more to do with God.

Each decision I had made became a bar to my prison cell; and while I felt I was now free from my father's domination, I was as captive as any jailbird, alone and isolated in my misery.

I had no idea how to begin talking about what had happened. I was haunted but couldn't imagine just walking up to someone, tugging on their shirtsleeve, and saying, "Sit down for a couple of hours. I have a story to tell." On the few occasions when I attempted to explain what we did and how we lived, I was met with the blank look of someone who couldn't relate in any way to what I was saying.

I felt guilty if I said anything that left Dad and Mom looking bad. I was sure it was a sin to tell anyone what had happened to Sammy. The Bible tells us to honor our father and our mother, and I feared I would dishonor Dad if I snitched on him. I was also afraid if I told anyone about our ordeal, Dad would be arrested for not providing medical care for Sammy when he was dying or for not helping Martha, who at the age of fourteen still couldn't talk or use sign language.

I also felt cheated. Everything others took for granted had never ever been given to me. I believed the world owed me what Dad had forcibly deprived me of, and I was going to get what was rightfully mine. Nothing and no one was going to stop me.

In silence and filled with anger, guilt, and fear, I began my next adventure—my spiritual journey home.

38

On the Road Again

By the time I was twenty-eight, I was already failing in my second marriage. Although I was fairly successful in a sales career, I was extremely unhappy and couldn't figure out why I was so miserable. I was also tormented by a full-blown ulcer and had to be very careful about what I ate—needing to eat frequent, small meals and empty my stomach every night before bedtime so I could sleep. And I still hadn't told anyone about the ordeal I had endured as a child. Oh, I had shared a few of the more traumatic experiences from time to time, but I had never revealed them in depth to anyone.

In the spring of 1983, at the urging of John Kitch, a man I viewed as a mentor, I attended an introduction to the est Standard Training (a model for living designed by Werner Erhard to help individuals transform their lives). Debi, his daughter and my now-best friend, had participated in this course as a part of her job training. It had changed her life, and he decided it might change mine.

At the time, est was a two-weekend affair, going from nine o'clock in the morning into the wee hours of the next morning. My biggest fear in taking est was that I would be allowed only one meal a day—and not until six o'clock each evening.

On the first three days of est sessions, we ended around two in the morning, got a few hours sleep, and were back at it by nine o'clock the following morning. By Saturday of the second weekend, my ulcer was completely gone away. That Sunday, we went from nine in the morning through the night and were unleashed on the world Monday morning at five-thirty. It was so late I didn't even go to bed—I went home, showered, and went straight to work.

I won't even attempt to describe est—it would be like trying to tell you what a maguacata tastes like—you just have to experience it. From a spiritual perspective, it was the most comprehensive examination of the temporal mind I had ever been exposed to. After three long days of delving into the nature of our "identity"—who we considered ourselves to be—I came to a moment on the fourth day where the internal dialogue stopped. It just stopped cold. The little voice in my head was silent. You know, that little voice? The one that's saying "What little voice? I don't hear no little voice." *That* little voice. When it stopped, I was no longer my story, my body, my opinions, my points of view, my past, my aches and pains, my fears, my gender, my race—I was none of those things. And I was still here—just being. Like a near-death experience, that moment changed everything. In that moment, everything was possible.

Of course, the internal dialogue started up again because it is relentless, endlessly explaining the world around us, and when I raised my hand and shared that it was nice to be free of the little voice, everyone laughed. And I realized later that it was the little voice, now on loudspeaker, that was sharing it was nice to be free of the little voice.

The est experience was very intrusive; there was a lot of conversation about "what happened" versus "the story or interpretation of what happened"; and as I went through the program, I caught glimpses of the power in that particular distinction.

I began to see that the traumatic events of my past were damaging, but not nearly as devastating as the decisions I had made about myself as a result of having experienced those events.

For example, when Sammy died, I decided I was a murderer. Perhaps more accurately, I *became* a murderer. It wasn't that I decided I was a murderer in the normal sense of a well-thought-out decision, but that I became a murderer in the emotional sense. It sort of crept up on me as I searched for answers to the question: *Why did Sammy die?* I subconsciously adopted the identity and began to wear it like a garment. It became the air I breathed and the water I swam in. As we peeled those layers back, I got to the place where I could take ownership of the fact that I had sentenced myself, as a judge might sentence a criminal, guilty of murder.

And crimes must be paid for.

Another important idea est hammered home was that our relationship to each parent is the lens through which we see, and therefore relate to, every other person in our lives. So to whatever degree I was incomplete, had unfinished business with my dad, to that same degree I was incomplete with all men; and to whatever degree

I was incomplete with Mom, to that same degree I was incomplete with all women. With that realization, I began the process of forgiving my father. I had to forgive him, or I would remain spiritually dead.

But I didn't want to forgive my father.

I saw him as a cruel, inhumane jerk. I feared and reviled him; and yet, I also admired him.

I thought he was the worst human being who had ever lived; and yet, I saw him as brilliant.

In my mind, he still represented God—a confusing, angry, violent, vindictive, paranoid God.

I once read an article about a study of approximately eight hundred subjects who were each asked to complete two statements: "Describe God," and "Describe your father." In the vast majority of the cases, the two descriptions were almost identical.

I couldn't see God because all I could see was my father.

In 1984, I began training in earnest to lead est programs. The first step was the Guest Seminar Leader Program—a six-month boot camp for cleaning up my life. There were four weekend sessions during a six-month span and homework and volunteer assignments between each of the sessions.

The second weekend was about my life and how much of my attention and energy was consumed with incompletions—unfinished business. The homework between weekends two and three was extensive. I was to pay all unpaid bills; clear up any incompletions with family and friends; apologize and make right any wrongs done to others; clear up any issues with the IRS, say, unpaid or unfiled taxes; clear up or make agreements to pay credit cards and other debt; handle any unresolved issues with the law, such as outstanding warrants and even unpaid parking tickets; balance my checkbook; clean up and keep clean my car and home; make my bed every morning; begin a fitness program; upgrade my wardrobe; and generally leave every space I touched in better condition than when I arrived.

This included bathrooms. We were to leave all bathrooms cleaner when we left than when we arrived, which sometimes meant cleaning a filthy public restroom from top to bottom.

Being somewhat of a germaphobe, I particularly objected to this practice; but I took it on anyway and found, to my surprise, that when I cleaned a public restroom, I always felt clearer in my thinking. Somehow, it was an opportunity to embrace humanity with all its flaws, and this reduced my anger toward others and increased my generosity and spirit of contribution.

It was also during this time I interviewed for a course called The Nature of Reality. This was an eight-weekend course, completed over the period of a year, designed to get me out of my own way regarding my vision.

The interview process was startling. Lynn Carter, a somewhat eccentric woman who drove a perfectly restored 1930s Porsche and smoked tobacco from a tiny pipe, asked me what my vision was. Why should she invest eight weekends of her time training me if I wasn't up to something that would alter the world?

The interview went something like this:

"What is your vision?"

"Huh?"

"What are you up to in life?"

"Huh?"

"Don't say '*huh*'! What are you up to contributing to life? When you open the morning newspaper, what immediately interests you? What do you gravitate toward? Where are you on your own way?"

I wasn't really expected to know the answers to all those questions right off the bat—it was an inquiry. However, when she asked me the question, "What is your promise to God?" the long-forgotten memory of my vision at age eleven to bring thousands of people to the God of Love came rushing back to me, and I burst into tears.

I had found a long lost friend, and I began to work on that.

⁓⁕⁓

Although I experienced much relief from est, I still found myself unable to tell my story. I could relate bits and pieces of it, but most of the really rough stuff was still hidden within my heart. For one thing, I didn't know how to start. Sometimes I would begin telling a story, only to look into the eyes of the listener and see they really had no idea what I was talking about, and then I would give up. Besides, I was so accustomed to putting on a positive face about life that I didn't want to burden anyone with my pain.

Another reason I couldn't talk about it was every time I revealed too much about Sammy's death, I felt I was betraying Dad. I hated Dad...and I loved Dad, and I somehow hoped that one day I could make peace with him, and talking about the things he had done filled me with guilt. So I just kept quiet.

I continued to participate heavily in the est organization, however. I couldn't get enough of the relative freedom I was experiencing as I took the courses and seminars. In fact, within a few years time, I was leading many of the programs.

One evening, I went to the movies with one of the est instructors. Nancy Arvold was a powerful course leader and had been a family therapist before going on staff with Werner Erhard, the man who created est. She and I had become friends.

We settled on a movie called *The Mosquito Coast*, starring Harrison Ford. The film tells the story of a family, led by an inventor with a genius IQ, that moves to Central America to get away from an impending war (which exists only in the mind of this opinionated and somewhat mad inventor). He is inflexible, insufferable, angry, and paranoid. He belittles others and dominates his wife and children.

I won't spoil the movie for you in case you haven't seen it; but as I watched the film, I became more and more agitated. *There he is! That is my father!* I had never been able to describe him; and there he was, right up there on the silver screen.

As the movie progressed, Nancy kept looking over at me as I reacted to the somehow familiar scenes. When the story had unfolded and came to its climactic finish, I sat sobbing and exhausted while the credits rolled.

I had completely fallen apart.

Nancy turned to me and said, "We need to talk, huh...?"

We went to her house, and she made me some tea, and I told her the whole story. It was the first time I had been able to tell it out loud. I was thirty-two years old.

I would like to say that in that moment I was healed, but that's not how it happened.

I began dealing with the events of my childhood in earnest; and as I began to open up about what had happened in my childhood, I was more and more able to forgive my father for the things I was holding against him. And as I forgave Dad, my relationship with God became more available. The more I could see Dad as a fallible human being, the more compassion I felt for him, and the more I could distinguish Dad from God, paving the way to a more powerful relationship with Him.

But my God remained an impersonal being who couldn't possibly care about me.

I was still a murderer.

39

Redemption

Another marriage and two careers passed. By 2002, I had forgiven Dad and Mom and everyone in my childhood who had done anything to hurt me. I had done a few sessions of EMDR, a type of trauma therapy, on some of these issues and that had helped a lot. I was successful in my career as director of admissions for several proprietary schools and leading seminars for Landmark Education. The stomach ulcer no longer tormented me, and I was happily married to my fourth wife, Melissa.

But I was still a long way from peace.

Although I had forgiven all the hurts of my past, I was still a victim of it. I blamed all my failures on my childhood and credited all my successes as victories despite my experiences. I realized that as long as I was not the author of my life and had not taken responsibility for it, I was still its victim; and as long as I was victimized, I could never be free. It is impossible to be a victim and at the same time live in gratitude.

I still believed God had let me down. *How could God have taken Sammy? What were His reasons? Why had He allowed me to live in such a manner? Was it necessary for me to eat grasshoppers or food with maggots or watch Boy be brutally killed? Did I really have to be kicked around by my father? Why would a loving God let me go through all that?*

I realized that with God, I was going to have to go through the same process I had with the people in my life that I resented and who had hurt me. I had to bring my pain to Him in prayer, identify the resentment, look at what it cost me, look at my part in it, and forgive Him. Step by step.

What emerged from that process was a story—or possibly a revelation. In this story, when I was still in the spirit world before I was born, God and I made a deal. The deal was I would be born into my family and go through my experiences so that I would be better able to help others who endured traumatic experiences; and in that process, I would find my way and help others find their way back to our Creator.

It was a good story; and even though I couldn't say if it was true, it empowered me to let go of the pain and poverty of my childhood. I was no longer a victim of it or a victim of God, and my vision had almost come full circle.

I was still confused about doctrine. It seemed to me that what the churches were teaching was either too complicated and ritualistic, or too shallow and simplistic. Some churches I visited had rituals that were incomprehensible to me. Others were so permissive, it seemed they were telling me that all I had to do was believe in God and I'd be saved; and although this sounded attractive, I still had no peace and no power. I had always believed in God; but I needed saving now, moment by moment, not someday in the future.

I studied the early Church and attempted to imagine what the spread of the Good News must have been like. I realized that as the Disciples went from village to village, the illiterate peasants they encountered heard only the Gospel of say, John, while others heard only the Gospel of say, Matthew. And whereas some heard the Gospel through Thomas, others heard it from Andrew.

And I realized that my God of Love saved them with whatever fragment of Scripture or spoken word they had available to them; and the anointing of the Comforter, the Spirit of Truth, would continue to instruct them in all things. I saw that all they ever needed to know was in the Gospels. In fact, all they needed was to hear the words of Word-made-Flesh Jesus and believe, and they would be saved.

I have since come to understand that to "believe" means to "believe and follow." It means to obey the teachings of Jesus to the end. Jesus said, "Be faithful unto death and you will receive the crown of life." It is not a one-time decision but rather a daily and sometimes moment-by-moment decision. Jesus told the harlot caught in adultery, "Your sins are forgiven," but He also said, "Go and sin no more." My walk with Jesus became a now, now, now thing.

But I was still looking for the power.

Gandhi said, "If you want to find yourself, lose yourself in the service of others."

Mother Teresa said, "If you want to change the world, go home and love your family."

Jesus said, "The harvest is plentiful, but the laborers are few."

I became more directed to the presence *of* God rather than the belief *in* God. I saw my mission as one of action rather than just conviction because "faith without works is dead." I decided to leave the hammering out of doctrine to smarter people, and I asked God to direct my thinking and my actions. I told God that I just didn't know what He wanted me to do and teach. I prayed: *Just give me the truth!*

Then the thought came to me: *start with the basics.*

When Jesus was asked what the most important commandment is, He told us to love our God with all our heart, mind, soul, and strength and to love our neighbor as ourselves.

That sounded like a good start. I could commit to that.

Then I wondered, *how do I love my God with all my heart, mind, soul, and strength?*

I was directed to the parable of the sheep and the goats, where Jesus tells us that inasmuch as we feed the poor, give water to the thirsty, clothe the naked, and visit those who are sick and in prison, we do this to Him. And I realized that the way to love God is to love His children. So I rededicated my life to that vision I had as an eleven-year-old boy and to the God of my innocent youth and decided that when I came to Him face to face on the day of reckoning, I would ask for His mercy and His blessing.

I looked around and saw everywhere God's children in need.

I saw people who had once known God and had strayed—much like I had—and lost the sunshine of His Spirit. These people needed to be led back to the fold.

I saw foster children who had been used and discarded like worn-out garments. They needed to be loved.

I saw drunks and drug addicts who were lost and afraid. They needed someone to hold their hands and help them walk through the "valley of the shadow of death."

And with each encounter, I found that because of what I had endured, I could listen unflinchingly to their stories and their pain and help them feel heard, perhaps for the first time in their lives. I discovered that I didn't have to be an eloquent preacher to do God's work. I could help them understand that no matter how bitter the betrayal they experienced, forgiveness is possible. I could help them remember the innocence of their youth. And I could perhaps guide them on a path to return to the bosom of our loving Creator.

One last thing.

When I rededicated my life to Yahweh and His Son Yeshua, I remember turning to my wife Melissa and saying, "One of these days, I'm gonna have to deal with the alcohol."

Alcohol had become my master.

What started off as a beer once in awhile had turned into a torrent of alcohol poured down my throat. Over the decades, my drinking had progressed to the point where I didn't remember how I got to bed each night or what I had said to those around me.

Two years after rededicating my life to Yeshua, I was feeding, clothing, and housing fifteen young men and women who had been through the foster care system and needed help. None of us were sober. I was attempting to do God's will and help those kids and spread the Word, and I was a falling-down drunk.

The day came when the bottom fell out. I lost the ministry; the full-time job I was working to support those kids; a house I had built with my own two hands; and Melissa, who had had enough of my drunken, unchecked anger, walked out, and filed for divorce.

Up until that point, I was still running mostly on self-will. I still saw God as a kind of executive coach who would help me achieve my goals, rather than my

Father who was the sole teacher and director of my life. Finally, my willpower was bankrupt. I was beaten and destroyed. I fell on my knees and asked God to help me and take over my life. I surrendered my life completely to His will and direction.

On that day, the words of Jesus kept going through my mind, "Love not the world or the things of the world." On that day, I put Him in charge and sought His will for me daily. That day was the day I was born again.

Most people don't realize that the Twelve Steps came straight out of The Sermon on the Mount and the Book of James. The Twelve Steps are a practical, step-by-step way to follow the teachings of Jesus of Nazareth.

I got a sponsor and diligently worked the steps. As I worked through the program, practicing the steps, the pain I was still suffering began to fade away. The first time I had a moment of serenity I was about six months sober. I was driving to Houston with my windows down. The radio was turned up full blast, and I was singing at the top of my lungs to Pink Floyd's *Comfortably Numb*.

Singing and crying...crying tears of joy because my God Yahweh had rescued this wretch, and I was His son, and He was my Father, and that helpless child never had to cry again over anything he had experienced in this life. And that fleeting glimpse—that vision from so long ago—was as bright as lightening in my hands. I was forever free from my sentence.

Today, I am seldom ill at ease. My days are filled with purpose. I am busy in service to my God and His children.

As of this writing, I have not had a drop of alcohol in eight years…and I still clean public restrooms.

Epilogue

I started writing this book countless times over the past thirty years. I tried to find a point to it, a theme, some way it could make a difference. I have written it as a villain—a role I have tried on all my life to see if it fit. I have written it as a victim—using my past to justify my countless failures. I have written it as a victor over the wounds and scars of my past. I have attempted to put a timeline around it, to soften Dad's role in it, and to elevate Mom's.

I have written it in third person, as an observer, if you will, and I have attempted to write it anonymously. I considered the consequences this book might have had on my father while he was still living, and on my mother, who recently passed away. I have considered the effects it may have on my siblings and my children and on my nieces and nephews who knew and loved Dad. I have attempted to write it with the intention of publishing it and having it become a financial success, and I have tried to write it as a way of healing my broken self.

And as often as I have attempted to write my story, I have rejected writing it. Because I didn't want to spend the rest of my life thinking or talking about it. Because I didn't want to dishonor my father and mother in any way. Because I hadn't achieved success yet—whatever that is—and I felt it had to be successful—a story that would inspire others to overcome their own adversity. Because who would want to read this god-awful story anyway? And finally, I have rejected writing it because in some ways, it was just too damned painful to remember these incidents and recall the details. Many times, after writing a chapter, I would fall into deep depression for weeks or months. After writing one particular story, I was unable to write for over two years.

Yet, over the decades that span my adult life, people kept telling me. "Write your book!"

And so I have persevered. But not without asking myself: *Will this be too painful to read? Will my*

*stories cause readers to go into their own depression?
Will they somehow be driven away from God? Will they be
left hating my father and not getting the bigger picture?
How will this book affect their relationship with me?
Will I be shunned as someone with so much psychological
damage as to be considered a danger? Will I be judged as
weak, fatally flawed, ungrateful, full of excuses, or self-
indulgent?*

⟿⟡⟿

In writing this book, I have done my best to present the
events accurately. I have also attempted to arrange them
chronologically. But in telling these stories as I
remember them to siblings who were there, new facts
come to light, new ways of looking at events are
revealed, and much of what I have written about
happened simultaneously. In many cases, I have nothing
to reference them against, such as a place we lived or a
birthday party. We lived in a car. We rarely had birthday
parties. Our birthday cakes, more often than not, were
baked in a folding oven on a Coleman camp stove on a
cement table at a roadside park. (Thank you, Mom.) We
were not always in school, and I don't remember the
countless gas stations, water holes, campsites, roadside
parks, state parks, backyards, side streets, construction
sites, and church parking lots we called home.

While writing this book, I asked Yahweh to guide me: *Did You give me my story to simply live it or to tell it? And if I tell it, what do You want me to write? Will it forward Your Kingdom here on earth?*

I have also questioned myself: *What are my motives in telling my story? To throw a lifeline to a struggling soul? Or to justify myself? Am I playing the sympathy card? Or is it His will?*

I may never know the answers to these questions; but sometimes, it is more powerful to live inside a question, as Werner Erhard said, than to attempt to answer it.

God may or may not approve; although, I suspect if you are reading this, He has allowed it to come to pass, thereby giving His tacit approval. In the end, I throw out my story to you—just as it is. And I trust you to sort it out for yourself and arrive at your own conclusions.

I pray you will derive something of value—a lesson, an inspiration, or at least be entertained by the stories, and I trust the Spirit of Truth to use these passages to forward God's Kingdom.

May Yahweh bless you.

Benjamin Moore
May 2017

Acknowledgments

I would like to acknowledge the many people who made this book possible.

I acknowledge Patricia Ann Bradley, my mother, for teaching me to love unconditionally, and Charles Loren Moore, my father, for teaching me about faithfulness and perseverance. I acknowledge my siblings, Daniel, Althea, Ruth, Martha, and Samuel for holding my hand and accompanying me through this journey.

I am eternally indebted to Werner Erhard for creating the est Training and The Landmark Forum, both programs that enabled me to transform my relationship to my life from one of survival and victimhood to one of mastery. Werner Erhard is the most amazing human being I have ever met. I acknowledge the countless instructors who taught me the principles of Transformation along the way.

I am grateful for the people who have walked hand in hand with me through portions of my life: Tom Cheeley, Carlos Navarro Guzman, John and Debi Kitch, Celia, Brenda, Luz, and Melissa, those beautiful women who endured my insanity.

I acknowledge my sponsor, Marc, who seemed bright and cheery no matter how late I called. I acknowledge all my Twelve Step brothers and sisters who kept me alive through the valley of the shadow of death.

A special thanks to Patrick Hensley, my friend and co-worker, who introduced me to his mom, Cheri Lomonte, who read my book and decided the world needed to read it, too. A special thank you goes to Sheila Setter, my genius editor. Together, these two women have loved this book into existence.

Above all, I give all glory to my Master and sole teacher Yeshua for illuminating my way throughout this adventure. May Your words not come back void.

Works Cited

Scriptural References

Scriptural quotations appearing in this book come from the Holy Bible, King James Version (KJV) and New King James Version (NKJV), and in some cases, are paraphrased from memory.

Growing up and reading in Dad's services, I read the Bible in Spanish. For reference purposes, the actual English Scriptural passages are cited here by Bible chapter, verse(s), and version. Citations have been verified at Bible Gateway https://www.biblegateway.com

Chapter 1

Page 4: From that time Jesus began to preach, and to say, Repent: for the kingdom of heaven is at hand.—Matt. 4:17 (KJV)

Page 4: He who loves father or mother more than Me is not
worthy of Me. And he who loves son or daughter more than Me
is not worthy of Me.—Matt. 10:37 (NKJV)

Chapter 14

Page 58: To deliver such an one unto Satan for the destruction of
the flesh, that the spirit may be saved in the day of the Lord
Jesus.—1 Cor. 5:5 (KJV)

Page 58: That ye may be the children of your Father which is in
heaven: for he maketh his sun to rise on the evil and on the
good, and sendeth rain on the just and on the unjust.—
Matt. 5:45 (KJV)

Page 58: Therefore if thine enemy hunger, feed him; if he thirst,
give him drink: for in so doing thou shalt heap coals of fire on
his head.—Rom. 12:20 (KJV)

Page 58: 21 If thine enemy be hungry, give him bread to eat; and if
he be thirsty, give him water to drink:

22 For thou shalt heap coals of fire upon his head, and the Lord
shall reward thee.—Proverbs 25:21–22 (KJV)

Page 59: But God said unto me, Thou shalt not build an house for
my name, because thou hast been a man of war, and hast shed
blood.—1 Chron. 28:3 (KJV)

Page 77: The story of the prophet Nathan telling David that his
son will build God's temple.—2 Sam. 7:1–29 (KJV)

Page 78: The story of Elisha and the two bears.—2 Kings 2:23–25
(KJV)

Chapter 34

Page 156: Now when the sun was setting, all they that had any
sick with divers diseases brought them unto him; and he laid his

hands on every one of them, and healed them.—Lk. 4:40 (KJV)

Page 156: And great multitudes came unto him, having with them those that were lame, blind, dumb, maimed, and many others, and cast them down at Jesus' feet; and he healed them.— Matt. 15:30 (KJV)

Page 156: And I will give unto thee the keys of the kingdom of heaven: and whatsoever thou shalt bind on earth shall be bound in heaven: and whatsoever thou shalt loose on earth shall be loosed in heaven.—Matt. 16:19 (KJV)

Chapter 39

Page 193: Fear none of those things which thou shalt suffer: behold, the devil shall cast some of you into prison, that ye may be tried; and ye shall have tribulation ten days: be thou faithful unto death, and I will give thee a crown of life.—Rev. 2:10 (KJV)

Page 193: The story of the woman caught in adultery.—Jn. 8:1–11 (KJV)

Page 193: 35 And Jesus went about all the cities and villages, teaching in their synagogues, and preaching the gospel of the kingdom, and healing every sickness and every disease among the people.
36 But when he saw the multitudes, he was moved with compassion on them, because they fainted, and were scattered abroad, as sheep having no shepherd.
37 Then saith he unto his disciples, The harvest truly is plenteous, but the labourers are few;
38 Pray ye therefore the Lord of the harvest, that he will send forth labourers into his harvest.—Matt. 9:35–38 (KJV)

Page 194: 14 What doth it profit, my brethren, though a man say he hath faith, and have not works? can faith save him?

15 If a brother or sister be naked, and destitute of daily food,

16 And one of you say unto them, Depart in peace, be ye warmed and filled; notwithstanding ye give them not those things which are needful to the body; what doth it profit?

17 Even so faith, if it hath not works, is dead, being alone.

18 Yea, a man may say, Thou hast faith, and I have works: shew me thy faith without thy works, and I will shew thee my faith by my works.

19 Thou believest that there is one God; thou doest well: the devils also believe, and tremble.

20 But wilt thou know, O vain man, that faith without works is dead?

21 Was not Abraham our father justified by works, when he had offered Isaac his son upon the altar?

22 Seest thou how faith wrought with his works, and by works was faith made perfect?

23 And the scripture was fulfilled which saith, Abraham believed God, and it was imputed unto him for righteousness: and he was called the Friend of God.

24 Ye see then how that by works a man is justified, and not by faith only.

25 Likewise also was not Rahab the harlot justified by works, when she had received the messengers, and had sent them out another way?

26 For as the body without the spirit is dead, so faith without works is dead also.—Jas. 2:14–26 (KJV)

Page 194: 36 Master, which is the great commandment in the law?

37 Jesus said unto him, Thou shalt love the Lord thy God with all thy heart, and with all thy soul, and with all thy mind.

38 This is the first and great commandment.

39 And the second is like unto it, Thou shalt love thy neighbour as thyself.

40 On these two commandments hang all the law and the prophets.—Matt. 22:36–40 (KJV)

Page 194: The story of the Son of Man gathering all the nations and separating them one from another, as a shepherd divides his sheep from the goats.—Matt.25: 31–46 (KJV)

Page 195: Yea, though I walk through the valley of the shadow of death, I will fear no evil: for thou art with me; thy rod and thy staff they comfort me.—Ps. 23:4 (KJV)

Page 197: 15 Love not the world, neither the things that are in the world. If any man love the world, the love of the Father is not in him.

16 For all that is in the world, the lust of the flesh, and the lust of the eyes, and the pride of life, is not of the Father, but is of the world.

17 And the world passeth away, and the lust thereof: but he that doeth the will of God abideth for ever.—1 Jn 2:15–17 (KJV)

Other Works

Chapter 2

Davis, Linda. *The Children of God—The Inside Story.*
Grand Rapids, MI: Zondervan Publishing Company, 1984.

Chapter 11

Dead Sea Scrolls. http://dss.collections.imj.org.il

Chapter 35

Handel, George Frideric. *Messiah.* 1741.

Chapter 37

TCK World. "Dr. Ruth Hill Useem—the
sociologist/anthropologist who first coined the term 'Third
Culture Kid' (TCK)." www.tckworld.com/useem/home.html

Chapter 38

Werner Erhard. "The est Standard Training."
www.wernererhard.net/standardtraining.html

Landmark. "Seminar Leaders Program."
www.landmarkworldwide.com/advanced-programs/leadership-
and-assisting-programs/the-seminar-leaders-program

Werner Erhard. "The Nature of Reality."
Note: This was a course taught by Werner Erhard and
Associates. When Werner retired from the company, he sold all
his technology to his former employees who created Landmark
Education. They retired it and replaced it with the Wisdom
Course, led by the same instructors. While they own the rights
to the course, they have retired it.

The Mosquito Coast, directed by Peter Weir (1986; Burbank, CA:
Warner Brothers).

Chapter 39

EMDR Humanitarian Assistance Programs. "What is EMDR?"
www.emdrhap.org/content/what-is-emdr

The Landmark Forum. "Landmark Education: Define What's
Possible." www.landmarkworldwide.com

Alcoholics Anonymous. "The Twelve Steps and Twelve
Traditions." www.aa.org/pages/en_US/twelve-steps-and-twelve-
traditions

Pink Floyd. 1980. *Comfortably Numb*. Columbia Records.

Made in the USA
Monee, IL
23 June 2020